Twenty Miles Per Cookie

9000 Miles of Kid-Powered Adventures

Nancy Sathre-Vogel

www.familyonbikes.org

Twenty Miles Per Cookie
9000 Miles of Kid-Powered Adventures

Published in the United States by:

Old Stone Publishing

ISBN 978-0-9837187-2-7

To my boys — all three of you. You light up my life.
NSV

Table of Contents

Pipe Dreams and Harebrained Schemes

"Daryl!" I shouted. "Daryl! Where are you?" I called into the darkness, panic rising with each passing moment. Completely, totally, and utterly exhausted, I wandered around the forest in pitch blackness searching for my little boy. "Daryl!" I sobbed. "Daryl! Where are you?"

This family bike trip had seemed like such a good idea a few months back when we made the decision to take it. The trip seemed so *right* somehow. But now, it seemed wrong. All wrong. I was exhausted beyond belief and my precious son was gone – devoured by the darkness of a moonless night in the middle of the forest. My spirits were about as low as could get, my resolve had all but disappeared, and the joy had been sucked out of life. All I wanted was my son. I wondered just what kind of mother I was to yank her children out of school for a year, plop them on the back of a bicycle built for three, and drop out of society.

"Daryl!" I called.

Daryl's twin brother, Davy, looked at me with tears in his eyes. "What if we can't find him, Mom?"

"We'll find him, sweetie. We have to." I turned back to the pine grove where my son was wandering aimlessly.

"Daryl!" I sobbed into the all-encompassing darkness. "Answer me honey! Please answer me!"

After what felt like hours, I heard the little voice I had been praying for: "I'm here Mommy!"

Daryl emerged from the blackness and, as I fervently hugged my son, I thought back to the day this whole journey had begun and about all the days that were coming. In so many ways, the trip just wasn't worth it. Losing your child is every parent's worst nightmare, and my eyes had just been opened to the possibility. Somehow I hadn't even considered that prospect. I had thought about our journey for so many hours, and yet had never considered the disastrous consequences of simple mistakes.

It could so easily happen – Daryl had simply gotten lost on his way back to the campsite from the bathroom. What else could happen? We were so exposed, so vulnerable. We were out in the open, bared to every sort of element Mother Nature could throw at us. We would fight traffic and cross deserts. We would get sick. We would get lost. Maybe we should turn around and go home.

And yet there was another side of the equation – the "living your dream" part of it all. The romantic idealism residing in some long-since-buried part of me that refused to give up the ghost and go away. I tried to send it away. Many times, in fact. When my husband, John, and I came back to the US after our year-long bike trip through the Indian subcontinent sixteen years ago, I tried to settle down. I tried to live life as other Americans do.

But a couple years later, I accepted the fact (temporarily anyway) that we weren't cut out for the American Dream and headed out to teach in international schools in other countries. We lived in Egypt, Ethiopia, Taiwan and Malaysia. We traveled – on bikes, boats, camels, elephants, buses and trains – in dozens of countries. Our twins were born five years after John and I moved overseas to live the expat life and they traveled with us for the first seven years of their lives.

Twelve years after leaving our home country to work overseas, we came back to America to give it another shot. "This time it'll be different," I told myself. "This time I've got two boys who will tie me down. I'm older and wiser, and more tolerant of the rat race. This time it'll be fine. It will be – honest!"

That lasted a grand total of fifteen months until John came home from school one day. It had been a tough day in the classroom – one of those days when he looked at all the teenagers in his class and thought *What kind of masochistic son-of-a-bitch am I? Why do I come to this classroom day after day only to be tortured and humiliated by these hormone factories on legs?* (To be fair, there are other days when we teachers are convinced we've died and gone to heaven, and we look at those people earning six-figure salaries and feel nothing but pity. But that's another day...)

John slumped into our house after that particularly rough day and collapsed into his favorite chair by the window. His eyes glazed over and I knew he wasn't looking at the lawn that desperately needed mowing or the barn that needed fixing. He was farther away. Much farther away.

"Nancy," he said. "I can't do this. I need to get away. I want to buy a triple bike and take off. Just me and the kids – out exploring the world. We'll be the three musketeers. We'll be Mr. Incredible and his children saving the world from destruction and injustice! We'll be Superman and Spiderman and the Incredible Hulk rolled into one! Oh yeah – and you can tag along too."

I started thinking about our life in Boise, Idaho; middle-aged parents with two boys comfortably nestled in a large house in a suburb with a couple of cars in the driveway. We got up early and headed off to work, dropping the kids at daycare on the way. We worked all day, and came home late. And then we collapsed into bed, utterly exhausted. Isn't that the American Dream? Isn't that the way it should be?

But the real question was: was it the way I wanted it to be? Was the American Dream the be-all and end-all? Was it the path to enlightenment and roadway to happiness? Would I, could I, be content with a big house in the suburbs and some cars? *Was that really what life was all about?*

3

My mind drifted back to those years when I was young and carefree. I had always lived life on the wild side, taken advantage of every moment, and never said no. I was a rainbow chaser and adventure seeker. I flew to Pakistan sixteen years ago with a man I barely knew, biked with him for twelve months through the toughest conditions known to mankind, and then married him. I had lived in five different countries and bicycled in many more. And yet now, one would barely recognize me as that girl. I wasn't a more mature version of her; I was somebody completely different.

Gone was my spirit of adventure. Gone was my spontaneous, spur-of-the-moment, jump-up-and-go attitude. In its place was a gentle, mousy kind of being with both feet planted firmly on the ground. My kids knew me as the quiet strength of the household. I wasn't exactly the life of the party, although I told stories of days when I was. They always looked at me in disbelief when I talked about those days.

Maybe we *should* take off and go. Maybe it wasn't such a ludicrous thing to do after all. Perhaps we didn't have to lie down and take middle age quietly. We weren't too old to go chasing rainbows and living life in the saddle! Maybe this wasn't all some pipe dream after all!

"Let's do it, John!" I said excitedly. My eyes had taken on a gleam, my shoulders had been thrown back, and my back was a little straighter. "Let's go! Let's quit our jobs and take off. After all, our kids will never be eight years old again. We've only got one chance at life – let's make it a good one! Let's throw caution to the wind and take off! Come on kids – hang on tight! We're in for the ride of a lifetime!"

Three months later John and I stood in the garage surveying our gear.

"Holy mother of pearl, Nancy! How do you expect us to get all this crap on the bikes?" John bellowed as he stood there gawking at the massive pile of stuff that somehow had to be stuffed, crammed, or cajoled into fitting on our bikes. "We've got to get rid of some of this junk!"

"What are we gonna get rid of?" I asked. "We can't ditch the tent or the sleeping bags. We'll need the sleeping pads to insulate us from the ground. There's the stove, but we need that unless you want to eat sandwiches every night for a year. A pot big enough for the four of us... spare bike parts... rain gear... What are we going to ditch? We're already down to only one change of clothing for each of us – we can't go any lower than that."

One way or another that ungodly mountain of all our earthly belongings ended up condensed into the proverbial mole hill. The towering heap ended up, by hook or by crook, balanced on our cro-moly frames or piled into the trailers behind them.

John and the boys would be riding a bicycle built for three. John, as the captain of the triple, would steer and shift the bike. Davy sat directly behind his father and Daryl was the caboose way in the back. I would cycle behind them on a single bike.

In time everything made sense. Within weeks, it all fell into place and every item we carried had its own special resting place in the saddle bags called panniers that were mounted on our bikes. Those first few days of the journey, however, were chaos. Absolute, complete chaos. We didn't know who had what or what was where, or which pannier or trailer anything happened to have been stashed in.

We had no idea which pocket the granola bars were in nor where the nail clippers might be hiding. All we knew was that we had a lot of stuff. A mountain of it to be exact. Our mornings were spent cramming, lashing, and buckling as we laboriously piled all that gear on our bikes. By the time we took off, you could hardly call our vehicles "bikes." Sure they each had two wheels, but beyond that... well, they bore little resemblance to what most of us picture when we think of bikes.

But we were ready. We had quit our teaching jobs, purchased a triple bike for John and the boys, and rebuilt my old bicycle. Our bags were packed and goodbyes said. There was no turning back; there was only a year of adventure ahead. A year to pedal at will, turn on a whim, and explore sunsets without end. Ah yes, we were ready – ready to tackle this great continent of ours with our children, ready to live and experience and grow beyond our wildest imagination. Ready to be pushed further than we had ever been pushed – and ready for magic.

Rabbit Bushes
and Shoe Trees

- - - 🚲🚲 🚲 - - -

"Mom!" Daryl shouted. "Hey, Mom! There's a historical marker!"

I pulled my eyes away from the road for a minute, wiped the sweat from my forehead, and realized he was right before refocusing my attention back on the hill I was attempting to climb. My legs pumped, my heart pounded, my lungs cried out for more air.

"Can we stop here and take notes, Mom?"

It took a second to wrap my mind around this one. An eight-year-old kid was asking to take notes? After twenty years in the classroom, that was a first. Third graders simply don't ask to take notes.

"Not right now, sweetie," I huffed. "We're running behind schedule and have to get to Letha tonight," I gasped, attempting to get another lungful of air. "There will be plenty more opportunities for note-taking later this year."

"But Mom!" Daryl protested. "You promised! You said you would teach us. You said you would be our teacher. You said we could take notes on historical markers. Please!"

"Yeah, Mom," added his twin brother, Davy. "You said we'd learn to take notes on the trip."

Two against one. It was clear there was no way I would win this battle. I surrendered and my eighty-pound two-wheeled rig ground to a halt. John and the kids rolled up on his utterly ridiculous fourteen-foot-long contraption and stopped beside me.

"You know, Nancy," John said as he wiped his sweat-soaked forehead. "We'll never make it around America if we keep stopping like this. Heck – we'll never even make it to Letha if we keep stopping like this. Do you know how far we've gone so far? We left home almost six hours ago and we've pedaled a grand total of twenty five miles! We've got to pick up the pace a little bit." He turned to his sons. "Kids, did you hear that? We just can't do this – stopping for a break every three miles. We need to keep pedaling! We'll stop here for school, but then we're cranking it to Letha. Understand?"

Davy and Daryl nodded their heads as they scrambled off their bike and scurried to my trailer to retrieve their school bags. As they ran toward the informational sign they called, "What do we do now, Mom?" while pulling out notebooks and pencils.

Taking a deep breath, I staggered toward the kids in the middle of the parking lot and started wondering if this journey was such a good idea after all. What was it that John had said just a few hours ago – before we left home, before it was too late?

"Do you *really* want to do this, Nance?" he had asked. "It's not too late to back out you know. All we need to do is take everything out of the panniers and put the bikes back in the garage. Nobody would even know we had planned it to begin with. After all, ya' gotta admit this is a pretty harebrained scheme."

He was right. We were two middle-aged parents safely ensconced into the typical American life. And we were about to throw it all away for *what*? To ride *bicycles* around North America with eight-year-olds? Were we nuts?

And now, just a few hours later, as I stood there on the side of the road in the blazing sun with two kids and their insatiable curiosity and I felt on the verge of collapsing and exhausted beyond belief after pedaling my bike up a minor (in comparison to what was coming) hill, I wondered if I had made the right choice. What was I thinking?

Did I think I was SuperMom? Could I really pedal my eighty-pound bicycle around North America while still having enough energy to be Mom? Could I manage all the shopping and cooking and washing dishes and setting up the tent and taking down the tent every day? Could I be the kids' teacher and mother on top of it all, or was I foolish to even think about it? Was I beyond the point of ludicrousness to even consider the possibility?

Yet somehow, deep down within, I knew the answer. Yes, there would be times when we would struggle. There would be times when we would think we couldn't go on. There would be times when life was more difficult than we could imagine. But it would be worth it. I just knew it would be. I wobbled over to my kids to sit down beside them.

Dear Grandma,

This is the first day of our trip. We started at our house. I packed my aliens, alien food, and a puzzle snake. We stopped at a winery and listened to music for a while. There were tons of mosquitoes. We stopped at a historical marker and took notes. We went 40.12 miles. We went through Emmett and climbed on a tank there. We had tortillas and cheese for dinner. I am excited to be on the road finally.

Love, Daryl

Crossing into a new state! Granted, it was only 60 miles from where we started, but exciting nonetheless.

The following morning we packed up our sleeping bags and took down the tent. John and I piled everything on our bikes and we rolled out onto the road once more. The kids were excited about seeing more of their country and John and I listened to their babbles as we cycled toward Oregon.

Oregon! A new state, albeit one only sixty miles from our home. The boys grinned from ear to ear as they posed for a picture at the sign welcoming us to our second state, then we pedaled until we found a park that allowed camping. Our plan had been to get a few more miles in but, truth be told, John and I were tuckered out. Our bodies weren't used to pedaling fully-loaded bikes.

We tumbled off the bikes and set up camp in the city park. Using a hose, we showered away all the sweat and sunscreen that had built up on our skin, then the boys charged off to the playground to scramble around on the monkey bars.

As much as I wanted the day to be over, it wouldn't be for ages still. I grabbed my small daypack from a pannier and headed off to find a grocery store. It was only our second day on the road and I knew it would take a while to get my body used to the demands of this bike touring stuff.

Still, my bum hurt and my leg muscles screamed when I tried to bend over to get canned milk off the bottom shelf in the supermarket – and this was only day two of the journey. I could only hope my body, at 46, wasn't too old to break in eventually.

"Sorry guys," I apologized as I handed my sons a bag of potato chips and a can of ranch dip a couple of days later. "This is all I have for breakfast." Their eyes lit up, not quite believing that their mother, the one who venerates all things good and natural and organic, would hand them a bag of chips for their morning meal. They hungrily dove in before I could change my mind. Changing my mind, however, was not an option. I had no other food to give them.

Our food stash was down to nothing and we had a long way to the next town. We had somehow managed to make a big miscalculation and there we were, in the middle of the eastern Oregon desert with nothing except a bag of chips from the local bar. There was no store within miles, no *nothing* within miles – except a bar that sold chips.

"We're in trouble, guys," I mumbled as I crammed another Lay's into my mouth. "It's a long way to the next town. And from what we've heard it's not much of a town."

Davy and Daryl weren't complaining. They had potato chips.

"I know these chips aren't the most nutritious thing you've ever eaten, but it'll have to do," added John. "There's nothing between here and Juntura. And when I say nothing, I mean nothing. We're going to have to pedal hard today, guys. The water bottles are full, but we have no grub at all – except a few bags of Cheetos. You understand that? No food. That means that if we don't make these thirty four miles, we're toast. Think we can make it?"

10

The boys nodded their heads as they crammed in more chips.

John and I dared not get our hopes up. We knew we couldn't continue on without something edible to carry on our bikes. From what we had heard, the prospects of finding portable food in Juntura weren't good. We climbed aboard our bikes and set off, hoping beyond hope we would find the provisions we so desperately needed.

Hours later we arrived, famished, into Juntura. As promised, there was a restaurant in town, but no store selling food we could easily carry. The boys figured they had died and gone to heaven as they hungrily downed hamburgers, but John and I ate them with knots in our stomachs. "What are we going to do about food?" John asked me.

We had fifty eight miles over two passes ahead of us – the first passes of our journey. It was hot, our bodies weren't used to the demands of bike touring, and we would be passing through desert. We had already seen enough of the desert to know there would be nothing but miles and miles of sage brush and sand.

"Okay. Let's consider options," I replied. We both knew there weren't any. "We could talk to the people here in the restaurant and ask them for something. Maybe we could just order a bunch of sandwiches and carry them with us?"

"Yeah right – that'll work real great. It's over a hundred degrees out. You think we can carry enough sandwiches for two days without them going bad?" We began to seriously reconsider the wisdom of cycling through this desert, and wondered silently just what the chances were of arriving back home alive.

Our eyes wandered out the window to the steady stream of RV's passing by. "What about..." I pondered. "Those RV's... They've got food." I headed out the door to see if I could flag down a passing RV to beg.

An older couple stood next to our bikes. "How are you folks today?" I asked.

"I've never seen a bike like this before. That's some machine," the man told me.

"Yeah – it is kind of like a rolling wagon train, huh?"

It was one of those conversations that meandered around like a creek snaking through the mountains, and we soon discovered just how small our world is. Their daughter was one of the other Grade 8 science teachers at our school – John's co-teacher.

"Hey listen," I said. "We're in a bind. A big bind. We need food, and can't continue on until we manage to get some."

Dorothy and Norm very willingly scoured their car and pulled out every morsel of food they could find. We stashed trail mix and bread and cheese into our panniers, strapped a Styrofoam container of leftover Mexican food to the top of my trailer, and pedaled away knowing our bodies wouldn't appear as desiccated piles of skin and bones out there on top of one of the passes in the middle of Oregon's no man's land.

We crawled at a snail's pace up the first pass we encountered, using every ounce of strength we had to propel our heavy cycles up the grade. "I don't know if I can do this," I complained as I huffed and puffed to get enough oxygen to fuel my leg muscles. "This is only the first of hundreds of passes we need to climb, and I'm dead. What were we thinking?"

"I don't know. I've never bicycled this slowly – ever. You'd think I could get up this measly hill after pedaling hundreds of thousands of miles all around the world. The say tandems aren't good on hills, but I never dreamed a triple would be this tough." John collapsed beside me as the kids scampered off to play in the desert.

The two of us looked at our bikes leaning against a rock. They were both stuffed to the max. My bike was bad enough – loaded down with four panniers and a trailer – but the triple was fourteen feet of sheer madness. The bike and all the stuff on it weighed nearly one hundred twenty pounds. Then there was another hundred forty pounds of kid piled on. That meant that John was hauling nearly three hundred pounds around America.

"This is tough," John mumbled. "We've only been on the road five days and already my shoulders are killing me. Every time one of the kids wiggles it sends sharp, stabbing pains shooting through my shoulders."

We lay on the side of the road for a while pondering the clouds floating gently across the clear blue sky and thought back on how wonderful these past few days had been. Sure, it had been hard. We were physically and mentally exhausted. Our bodies cried out in protest at the punishment that had suddenly been thrust upon them, but there was something wonderful about it all too. All this time together – just us and the kids. It was a marvelous adventure and one we couldn't imagine quitting. Not yet anyway.

"I don't know how we're going to do it, but we'll never make it if we sit here complaining all day. Let's get to the top of this blasted hill." Coaxing the boys away from their newfound playground and back on the bike, we continued up.

"What the hell is that" questioned John a while later when he spotted a bizarre tree up ahead. "Is that all that's left of hundreds of poor travelers like us who perished our here like we're gonna do? All that's left is their shoes?"

"It's a shoe tree!" shouted Daryl.

"Yeah, it's a shoe tree! It sprouts shoes like leaves!" added Davy.

We ground our way up to the tree, sweat pouring off by the bucket-load, and stood looking at the not-quite-dead tree with hundreds of pairs of shoes hanging on it – big shoes, little shoes, new shoes, old shoes, sandals, sneakers, boots... You name it, they were hanging there.

"What do you think, guys? Why are those shoes hanging there?"

The Shoe Tree - There were hundreds of pairs of shoes of all shapes and sizes hanging from this tree.

Stinky Meat and the Shoe Tree

By Davy & Daryl

As we were riding we saw a shoe tree. This is why we think it is there: There is a monster named Stinky Meat. He lives in the mountains. One day four explorers were exploring a cave. The monster is usually small, but when he's right in front of someone during the week he turns big and eats them. So he ate one explorer. The rest of the explorers went back and told some shoemen. Little did the explorers know that Stinky Meat was following them. Stinky Meat was sort of kind, so he made a deal with the shoemen. The shoemen wouldn't tell anybody where the cave was and Stinky Meat would give them shoes. Now every time Stinky Meat eats someone, he takes the shoes and puts them on the tree. The shoemen go there to collect them. So the next time you buy a pair of shoes, think about the person who died.

After a rest day in Burns where we hung around the park and John and I did absolutely nothing and the boys kept themselves busy at the playground and city pool, we headed into the desert once again. I packed plenty of food for the two-day journey to Bend and we figured we could refill our water bottles in Hampton, forty-two miles of scorching hot desert away.

I grew up in Boise and like to think I'm used to the desert, but pedaling through the desert and driving through it are two entirely different animals. In a car, those forty two miles would have passed in about as many minutes. We would have sat in our air-conditioned cubicle and not even considered a need for water. But on bikes? That's a different story.

On bikes those miles were long – very long. And hot. Daryl discovered fairly early that the only shade he was going to find was under what he called "rabbit bushes." Every time we stopped, Daryl jumped off the bike and made a mad dash to the largest sage brush he could find and crawled under it. The rest of us sat in the blistering sun on the side of the road and basked in the glaring rays of the sun. And our water supply slowly dwindled away.

Ten miles from the tiny settlement of Hampton, I drank my last sip of water. My bottles were empty, and I knew I was in trouble. My well had gone dry.

"We still have enough water on the triple," John told me. "We'll be okay taking our time to get to town, but I'm concerned about you, Nancy. You always need so much more water than I do anyway, and it's hot today. I really think you need to take off. Just take off now and go – don't waste any more time. You need to get to water!"

Through the shimmering haze of my thirst-induced hallucination I saw a woman with a baby in one arm and a glass of water in the other. I reached out and grabbed the water, downing it in one gulp. Her arm reached out with a pitcher and I gratefully held out my glass for more. As I downed glass after glass of wonderfully cold refreshing water the haze began to lift and I began to wonder if this was truly a hallucination or if she really was standing there in front of me.

I remembered pedaling through the desert and running out of water. I remembered leaving my boys and taking off on my own in search of liquid refreshment. And I vaguely remembered seeing that big sign out front of the café – "Best Burgers in Town." But then it all got fuzzy... climbing off the bike and stumbling in... the water... the blast of air conditioning... the water... the smiling faces... the water... I guess you could say water is the essence of life. It was for me that day anyway.

I had just barely convinced myself that it was all real, not some bizarre hallucination when John and the boys tumbled in. "Water!" they cried. "Where's water?"

We were learning quickly that the learning curve of bike touring through deserts was steep. As it turned out, we had finally reached the apex and were on the downhill side of that particular learning curve – the cycling in the desert one.

Water sources and shade were few and far between in eastern Oregon. We took breaks while standing in the hot sun - not very relaxing at all!

There were other learning curves we hadn't mastered yet though. Regardless of how many miles we had toured in the past or how many nights we had spent in a tent, it just didn't seem like we could get ahead of the game. No matter how well-planned our trip was or wasn't, it just seemed like nothing went according to plan.

There was the basic stuff like food and water that we had to figure out. Then there were the strength and endurance issues on top of that. We were putting in sixty mile days and all four of us were just plain tuckered out

"I'm tired, Nancy," John mumbled as we took a break the next morning. "I'm exhausted, and my shoulders are killing me. A big butcher knife jabs into my shoulders every time the kids wiggle. I can't do it. I just can't. You've got to help me out here. I can't go on."

I took over as captain of the triple. The kids and I did okay, albeit a bit slow. John rode alongside us on my bike joking and laughing with the kids, encouraging them to pedal hard. And they did pedal hard – in spurts. We would all settle into a nice comfortable cadence, and then John would come up and say something and the kids started pumping like mad. I shifted to accommodate their burst of energy. Then shifted back down when they got tired.

"Last one to the campground has to cook dinner!" John shouted as he sped past us.

The boys rounded up a burst of energy and started cranking. I shifted. A few seconds later they petered out. I shifted back down.

"First one to the store gets an ice cream cone!"

It was wearing on my nerves. I was mighty tired of the irregular pace after captaining the bike for twenty five miles so when John came up, once again urging the kids on, I snapped. "Shut the fuck up would you?" I shouted.

And John shut up. For good. He refused to talk to me and rode way behind us. In short, he wanted nothing – absolutely nothing – to do with me. I can't say I blame him.

The kids and I set our pace. We pedaled. We took breaks under trees. At one point we even got out our mats and took a nap in the woods. And all the while, John was nowhere to be seen. He stayed behind us, being sure to keep an eye out to make sure he wasn't too far behind.

It was getting dark when we arrived into Bend after cycling sixty five miles that day. I wearily pulled into a store to call our friends when John rode by. My boys and I ran to the road.

"John!" I shouted, as I waved my arms in the air.

"Daddy! Daddy!" the boys yelled while jumping around trying to catch his attention. "Daddy! We're back here!"

John didn't see nor hear us, and simply continued on. The three of us jumped back on the bike and pedaled like mad to catch up with him. We pedaled like demons possessed, but he had simply vanished.

The sun had set and darkness was quickly settling in. I finally accepted the fact that John was lost. Or we were lost. I wasn't sure which. I called our friends to get directions to the campground, and that's when John rode by.

"Where the hell have you been?" John screamed. "A driver told me you were behind me, so I circled around to go back but you weren't there. What in the hell are you doing?"

The four of us set off together to get to the campground outside town and, thirty minutes later, pulled into the campground in complete darkness, absolutely exhausted after our longest day yet. We had no food and weren't about to climb back up the hill to get to the store. We decided to eat the last of our snacks for dinner and go to bed.

The boys and I had headed to the showers while John set up camp. Daryl finished showering first and wanted to return to our site. "Not a problem," I told him. "Do you know where we're camped?"

"Yep – hiker/biker site in Loop A."

And that was when Daryl got lost and I had reason to seriously question the wisdom of what we were doing.

Davy and I took a leisurely shower and ambled back to camp to discover – no Daryl. Panic set in. It was pitch black and the campground was enormous. I could just picture the little tyke wandering off into the woods to become some kind of tasty snack for a big bad wild animal. I set out in one direction with Davy in tow, while John headed another direction, both of us shouting his name into the darkness.

Eventually, I heard his little voice calling to me through the trees and, as I stumbled toward him in the dark, I couldn't help but feel indebted to God himself for returning my son to me.

That night I as I lay in our tent with Daryl snuggled up on one side and Davy on the other, I thought about all the quarrels and squabbles of the day. It was so trivial, and yet it had seemed like such a big deal at the time.

In retrospect, all that mattered was that we were together, the four of us, exploring America and learning together as a family. All that bickering? All that arguing? For what? I set my sights on a new day, resolving like never before to delight in the magic of time together as a family; of learning and growing together. Our journey was such a gift – and I wasn't about to throw it away quite yet.

By the time the end of June rolled around a mere ten days into our journey, I couldn't wait until winter darkness forced us off the road at a reasonable hour. The long summer daylight hours were dragging us down. Each evening we tried to go to sleep early, but it was difficult to sleep with the sun beating down on our tent. By the time the sun set and we managed to settle down, it was nearly 11:00 p.m. Every morning we wearily dragged the kids out of the tent bright and early in order to be on the road by 4:30. It was just so bloody hot later in the day and the only time we made any decent mileage was early – but that didn't give any of us much time to sleep.

"I'm tired, Mom," complained Davy one day as we pedaled along a beautiful country road.

"Me too," murmured Daryl. "I wanna sleep."

"I tell you what," John told them. "We're almost to Redmond. We'll stop there and take a break in the park, okay?"

"A long enough break that we can sleep?"

We arrived into Redmond and headed to the park so the kids could play.

They took one look at the playground, and another look at our laps, and made their decision lickety-split. They both climbed up on a lap and fell asleep. There we were – glued to the park bench by sleeping kids. And they showed no indication they would be awaking any time soon. Eventually we gave up and decided they really did need to sleep, pulled the mats off the bikes, and laid the kids down on the grass.

Figuring out a workable schedule was a chore. None of us wanted to go to sleep while it was still light, but we did want to take advantage of the morning cool – and therein lay the quandary. The boys wanted to sleep in late, play during breaks, and go to sleep after the sun set. John and I wanted to be on the road at first light. Could we ever find a compromise?

In time Mother Nature came to our rescue by making shorter days, but in the meantime, it was a daily battle and we never truly figured out a workable solution to the problem. We just stumbled on, knowing these long summer days would soon be a thing of the past.

Long summer days and early morning starts led to very tired kids. I couldn't wait for fall to come to provide some relief.

Those first few weeks on the road were filled with figuring out solutions to problems. Even though John and I had toured on our bikes a lot, there were always new problems to solve and creative solutions to be found. Touring with kids added a whole new dimension to the experience and somehow we never seemed to be able to foresee what was coming.

"Nancy!" John called out in the middle of the night when we were camped in the fairgrounds in Madras, Oregon. "Wake up! It's raining!" We scrambled out of the tent in the pitch black to put the fly on our tent. As I emerged from our nylon home I looked at the rain pouring from the sky and the multitude of odds and ends scattered about on the grass and I realized we were sorely unprepared for rain – in fact, we were about as unprepared as one could be. Our fly was about the only item we owned that was properly packed away. Everything else was receiving the full brunt of the rainstorm.

What had we been thinking? We had packed raingear to keep us dry while cycling in rain, but now our bikes were out in the deluge, with panniers and trailers standing wide open as if funneling water in was their primary job.

John and I scuttled about in the pouring rain trying to protect our gear the best we could, which was miserably poor given our circumstances. "Here – take this tarp!" called a young couple camped next to us. We spread the tarp over the bikes, hoping to protect the panniers a bit. Our sole flashlight, which was running dangerously low on batteries, barely illuminated all the gear strewn about. We picked up the best we could, stashed everything in the panniers and trailers, put the fly on the tent, and climbed back in to wonder how we would fare.

It didn't take long to find out, and the news wasn't good. In fact, it was downright dismal. By morning, the tarp had blown away and our panniers were soaked, along with everything inside them. The good news was that the tent held up well so we were dry inside. It was just that everything else was dripping.

All morning it rained. And rained. And our stuff became even more water logged. The four of us hung out in the tent reading books and playing cards. By noon the sun broke through, and we spread everything out on the tarp, which we rescued from the opposite side of the fairgrounds. We were lucky that nothing got ruined and we learned a very important lesson about preparedness. Our shopping cart held a big tarp the next time we visited WalMart.

The following day was one of those days when the mercury topped the century mark and a hill stretched in front of us unabated. John realized there was no way he could lug three hundred pounds of gear and little boys to the top.

"Okay guys, here's the deal," he announced to Davy and Daryl. "There's no way I can do this one by myself. You're gonna have to help. And by help I don't mean just letting your legs go around in circles. You're going to have to pedal like there's no tomorrow. You're gonna have to somehow find those body builder's muscles that I know are in your legs. You need to pedal hard, break a sweat, and be gasping for air. If you don't want to do that, get off and walk." Davy opted for the sweat and panting. Daryl opted to walk.

John and Davy quickly disappeared up the hill, while Daryl was left to fend for himself. I pedaled alongside him as he slowly made his way up the interminable hill, and his pace slowed until he was creeping slower than an arthritic turtle. I feared we would never crest the top of that bloody hill.

They say desperation is the mother of all invention, and she certainly drove me that day. I finally realized there was no way my son would make it up on his own volition. No way he would reach the summit upon his own two legs. I faced a very important decision: carry him up myself, or leave him behind for the coyotes. I put on my SuperMom persona.

"Put your helmet on, Daryl," I instructed. He looked around, thinking Daddy must have come back to rescue him, but Daddy was nowhere to be seen. He looked at me with one of those looks on his face – one of those *what in the heck are you saying?* looks. "Here." I handed him his helmet. "Put it on."

"Now, this is what we're gonna do. I need you to climb up here on top of my trailer. That's right, right there smack-dab on top of my sleeping bag and the jar of peanut butter. But see these wheels? Don't touch 'em. Pretend these spokes are boy-eating serpents whizzing past your face. Understand? Don't touch the spokes." Daryl nodded his head as he tucked his hands under his bottom.

"Ready?" I asked. Daryl looked at me with a newfound sense of wonder, realizing that I was the female version of his childhood hero.

A while later Daryl and I arrived at the top of the hill.

"Look at me!!" my son shouted as he approached his father and brother while perched upon his sleeping bag throne. "I'm King of the Hill!" He threw his arms up in victory, while I headed to a phone booth to change out of my SuperMom outfit.

We had been on the road for two weeks and Davy was done. He had decided enough was enough. Pedaling through the desert in 100 degree heat just wasn't doing it for him and he wanted to go home. He wanted to sleep in his own bed at night. He wanted to play with toys and watch TV and have his friends over. The bottom line was he was bored.

"Bored? Out here in God's country?" John asked when Davy complained of wanting to turn around. "How could you possibly be bored? I mean – there's tons to do. How could you want to go back home? Look at all there is to do out here."

"Yeah sure, Dad," Davy replied sarcastically. "What's here? Sure, there's a whole bunch of sage brush, but that's pretty boring. Back home I have toys and a trampoline. And I could be playing with my friends right now. That's a whole lot more exciting than riding a bicycle through this boring desert."

"Wait a minute, son," John told him. "Look at this! Look at all this sage brush – bush after bush of one of the most remarkable plants in Earth! These things can live with barely any water at all – how cool is that?"

"Yeah Dad, it's cool. It's real cool. Now can we go back home?"

"And look! You can pee on an ant hill! Where else are you gonna be able to pee on ant hills?"

"Yeah, that is kinda fun, but I still want to go home."

John and I were devastated. We were living the dream. We were biking around America and spending time with our boys. We were exactly where we wanted to be. But this, well, this threw a monkey wrench into our entire plan.

We had discussed our route for hours before setting out. We knew getting through eastern Oregon, with its miles and miles of barren desert, would be hard. We were fairly certain once we got to the coast where there would be new sights to see every day and exciting things to do and learn, things would be fine. But getting to the coast would be the hard part. It would be a few weeks of a tough grind with few distractions. This was exactly what we had feared.

"Pssttt... Davy, come here!" I whispered. I leaned down next to Davy and whispered into his ear. "I tell you what. If you hang in there and go with us, I'll take you to Disneyland when we get to southern California, okay?"

A big grin spread across his face. "Really?" he whispered back.

"Really," I promised.

"Okay, I'll go," Davy announced. And he jumped back on the bike with a smile. Apparently, there were times when I didn't even have to don my lycra outfit to save the day.

I doubted even my SuperMom powers could have helped Daryl though. He was tired. Very tired. He was so tired he could fall asleep on a bed of nails... or a rolling bicycle, whichever happened to be more convenient. Nothing could keep him awake. Every time we stopped he collapsed off the bike and curled up on the pavement, dead to the world. We would let him sleep a few minutes before dragging him up and propping him on his seat.

Some days were like that – climbing hills, fighting head-winds, trying to motivate one little boy, and propping up another's eyelids. Eventually we figured out how to make it all work and we settled into a comfortable routine, but those first few weeks were rough. The learning curve looked like it would never end.

"Here – take my house key. I'll be there in a few hours," Mary said as she handed us a key.

John and I were dumbstruck. We stood there looking at the house key in our hand, unable to respond. I looked at John as if to say, "Did she just hand us, total strangers, the key to her house?" He looked at me and nodded.

Mary in Portland, Oregon was our first encounter with a real Road Angel. Later in our journey we weren't quite so surprised when people reached out to help us in many ways, but at the time Mary handed us the key to her house, we had no idea what was to come.

We had arrived into Portland, our first big city, with all its masses of humanity and cars after a long day of fighting headwinds in the Columbia River Gorge. John white-knuckled his way through the city streets as we searched for a campground, only to discover there was some sort of ordinance against tents in Portland. The nearest place we could pitch the tent was seventeen miles away in Vancouver. Our options were few – we could sleep in the streets or get a hotel.

"Nancy, we can't do this, you know," John complained. "We'll be on the road for a year. A whole year. We've quit our jobs and have no paychecks coming in. We can't be checking into motels on a whim."

"I wouldn't exactly call this a *whim*," I retorted. "What are our choices? Yeah, I suppose we could sleep on the street with all the winos and druggies. That would put our boys exactly where we want them! I mean, there just aren't a whole lot of options right about now."

We began to fill out the paperwork for checking into a motel when a woman with long salt-and-pepper hair poked her head in the door. "Hi!" she smiled, "You probably don't remember me, but I saw you out in the gorge a couple days ago. I got you back on the right track that time you were lost. Anyway, I just happened to see your bikes out there, so decided to come in and say hi."

We explained our predicament. "You can camp at my house tonight if you want. I only have a small backyard, but it's big enough for a tent."

She gave us directions and was ready to head out to the meeting she was on her way to. And then she pulled out her house key and handed it to us. "I've never done this before," she said, "but I have a feeling I won't be burned."

Mary was just the beginning of our dealings with Road Angels. As stunned as we were by her generosity and trust, we were about to learn that in our moments of greatest need, a Road Angel would appear, sometimes in the most unlikely places. At each corner – each twist and curve in our road – they were there and waiting for us, waiting to add magic to our journey.

"Hey guys!" John shouted. "Look up there! Do you see what I see?"

Davy and Daryl leaned out to look around their father in front of them on the triple bike. "The ocean!" Daryl cried. "The ocean! We made it! The Pacific Ocean!"

"I want to go swimming! Can we, Dad? Please?" Davy begged.

Twenty-one days after we pulled out of our driveway, we caught our first glance of the Pacific Ocean. Her waters sparkled and shimmered in the sunlight, and we rejoiced in the sight. We had made it. We had survived the first leg of our journey.

Reaching the Pacific Ocean was a huge accomplishment for us!

We all knew this was the shortest leg, but the most difficult in many ways. We had needed to learn the ropes and figure things out. We had broken our bodies and minds into the idea of being modern day nomads. We had crossed the desert in searing heat. But we had made it. We had learned more than we ever dreamed, and looked forward to more.

Broadsided by Beauty

Three weeks on the road had changed us. No longer were we a ragtag mob living in chaos, but were well on our way to becoming a well-oiled machine. Each item we carried had found a home in our bags, and we had all discovered each other's strengths and weaknesses. We had learned to depend upon each other, knowing exactly which ways each could help.

Mornings were still a challenge as we passed through our routine of stuffing the sleeping bags, taking down the tent, and loading our bikes, but with all four of us pitching in our routine was streamlined into a forty-minute process. We fell into a rhythm, knowing exactly how far we could comfortably pedal in a day (not far), how often to take breaks (very often), and how much food to pack (a lot). In the evenings, each person had their chores and knew exactly what was expected. Squabbles were few as we relaxed and enjoyed each other's presence, celebrating the incredible gift we had been given.

We camped next to a small creek one evening and all four of us quickly pulled on our bathing suits for a refreshing dip in the cool water. As I sat in the shallow water watching my boys play, I was stunned by the changes in their bodies. Gone were the baby soft bodies they had sported when we pulled out of our driveway. Instead I saw rock solid muscles that hours of pedaling had developed and I couldn't help but wonder what other changes had been going on inside their bodies and brains.

We were on a roll until we woke up to find our tent floating in a massive puddle of water one morning. A new pond had sprung up at some point in the night, and decided its home would be the exact spot of ground where our tent sat. The four of us climbed out into the muck and stood staring at the puddle, wondering just what we were doing out there in the middle of the pond in the first place. After all, we had chosen this. We could have been sitting at home safely protected from deluges and unexpected ponds.

I suppose we could have turned it all around and exclaimed, "The tent's floating! Yeehaw!" After all, the only other option was even worse. If the tent didn't float, it would have meant all the water passed inside, and that would have been even more depressing than a floating tent. So we didn't complain too much – we were all warm and dry. But that didn't change the fact that it was one of those terrible, horrible, no-good, very bad days. It was raining. A lot. And our tent was sitting in a massive puddle of water. The boys and I packed up and walked into town to hang out at the library and update our online journal.

A few hours later a man walked up to me. "Hi Nancy! I'm taking you home!"

I looked at him like he was off his rocker.

"I just talked with John. He sent me here to get you and the boys."

I looked at him as though he had just declared himself to be a flying purple cow. "What did you say?" I asked.

"I just read on your journal that you guys were stuck up in the campground above Montesano, and I thought, 'I know where they are!' So I drove up there and waded through the muck until I managed to find John cozied up in your tent in the middle of a puddle. For some bizarre reason, he wants to stay with the tent, but he sent me here to find you and the boys. So – will you come stay with my wife and me tonight?"

I started to wonder if America's Road Angels had banded together to make our journey special.

The next few days were a blur of beautiful scenery, wonderful people, and icy swims in the Puget Sound. One morning we pedaled away from a campground for a short trek to the ferry for San Juan Island to spend a relaxing day with friends.

After what seemed like twenty miles, I stopped my bike. "This seems like a whole lot farther than the seven miles you said it was going to be," I mentioned to John.

"I know," he replied. "I'm not sure how far we've gone, but it sure does seem longer than it should have been."

We kept pedaling, wondering just when we would find the ferry dock. It had been a simple plan for a simple day − ride seven miles to the ferry, and be with our friends in a couple of hours. Should've been a piece of cake, but a month on the road had taught us a thing or two about who was in control − and it certainly wasn't us.

Finally we saw the sign: *Ferry Dock - 7 Miles.* Cripes! John and I looked at each other in wonder. Somehow, somewhere, we had missed a turn. And instead of taking a nice, easy, seven-mile jaunt over to the ferry, we did a whopping twenty-six mile loop of the entire island.

By the time we got to the dock, the ferry to San Juan Island was long gone.

We had a choice. Pedal back to the campground and wait until tomorrow, or jump on the ferry leaving immediately to Orcas Island. We opted for the latter.

A friend once told me the group of islands known as the San Juans were steeper than anything he had ever seen, and I don't doubt him. We set off to the campground and climbed up. And up. And up. Those islands popped out of the ocean and headed straight to heaven. I could have sworn Orcas Island was the stairway to heaven for the gods.

Round about dark we straggled into the campground and fumbled around getting organized for the night. By the time we finally collapsed into our sleeping bags we were exhausted. All four of us had been looking forward to an easy day and a relaxing evening hanging out with friends. Instead we ended up with yet another grueling day in paradise.

Hiking provided a welcome relief from the bicycles.

And paradise it was. Orcas Island enchanted and intrigued us with its diverse landscape of mountains, wooded countryside and spectacular vistas. In fact, we were so spellbound we couldn't drag ourselves away as planned, but spent a day hanging out, swimming in local lakes and sightseeing.

The next day we plunged back down the mountain to board the ferry to San Juan Island where we met our friends and enjoyed that relaxing evening after all. Our friend, Donna, dropped us off at the campground late at night and we were promptly lulled to sleep by the gentle ocean sounds.

Disappointment reigned as we reluctantly pulled out of the campsite the following morning. There we were – in the most spectacular camp spot on San Juan Island; *the* premier whale-watching site on the islands. And we hadn't seen a one.

We had hung around for hours hoping to see that distinctive tell-tale splash of water, but the whales remained elusive and we were forced to head out – the ferry wouldn't wait for whales.

As we pedaled along the coast toward the ferry dock, we kept our eyes peeled for the animals. Sure, we enjoyed the gorgeous rocky shoreline lined with blackberry bushes, but what we wanted to see were the massive magical creatures of the sea.

"Daddy! Look!" shouted Davy. "Out there – whales!" We all looked toward the water and, sure enough, spotted the little splashes from their blow holes. Silently, mesmerized by the magnificent sight before our eyes, we climbed off our bikes and stood there, transfixed. The whales, a pod of perhaps six or eight, frolicked in the waves directly ahead of us.

Daryl stood, awestruck, with the rest of us for about two minutes – until he discovered blackberries at his feet. "Heck with whales!" he said, "I'm gonna eat blackberries!" He dove into the bushes, leaving the rest of us to gaze at the incredible animals before us.

"Look, Nance!" John blurted a few minutes later. His outstretched arm pointed toward the top of a tall, solitary tree near the edge of the water. My eyes followed his arm until I saw it too – a bald eagle perched high in a tree. He sat watching over all of us as though he had been appointed guardian.

It was one of those incredible moments we never wanted to end: whales frolicking before us in the waves... blackberries at our feet... and a majestic bald eagle presiding over the ceremony. *Yes, this is why we're here. This is why we are taking this journey!*

Dear Grandma,

I was interviewed by a news reporter this morning because we are riding bikes around America. It is fun being famous. I flew a kite before we left the campground. I saw some whales. They were cool. We ate blackberries. We didn't eat the purple and red ones because they were sour. We took a ferry into Canada. It was fun on the ferry.

Love, Davy

The next couple days continued in that perfect mode. The scenery was lovely, cycling was easy and we couldn't have asked for better weather. We were in the groove and everything was going swimmingly. Until we got separated.

I sat in Humptulips wondering what could have happened to John and the boys. I waited. And waited. And waited some more. It just didn't make sense – they were only one minute ahead of me. Sixty seconds – and then they disappeared.

"We'll meet at Humptulips if not before, 'kay?" John had shouted as he pulled out of the campsite.

"That's fine," I called back. "I just need to strap on the tent and I'll be on my way."

It was only a minute or so before I jumped on my bike and headed out to catch up to John and the boys. I pedaled fast knowing they would be going slowly waiting for me.

Hmmm... I thought a couple miles later. *This isn't like them. They don't generally go this fast. I should have caught them by now.* I kept pumping, trying to catch up.

It started to rain. I pushed on. And all of a sudden there I was – in downtown Humptulips. Alone.

Now I've never claimed to be the brightest person walking the face of the earth, but I'm not the dumbest either. I had just cycled the entire length of that road and the boys weren't there. I knew they weren't behind me. Which meant, of course, that they had to be ahead of me. But I was where we were supposed to meet, and they weren't. *I suppose they could have gone right by,* I thought. *After all, it is a pretty small town and it would be fairly easy to miss if you were going fast.*

"Did you happen to see a great big bicycle built for three up there?" I asked drivers as they pulled up to the gas station I was waiting at.

Time after time, I got a negative response. "No – can't say I did!" they each told me.

My boys had vanished. Disappeared. Fallen off the face of the earth. Not even my SuperMom powers could bring them back – that only worked if I knew where they were to begin with. I sat down to consider all the options. They weren't ahead of me – I had asked numerous drivers and surely someone would have seen that massive machine lumbering along the highway. They weren't behind me – I would have had to pass them to get here. Could they have taken a wrong turn? There weren't any turns. Could they have stopped for a break? I would have seen them. Or would I? I suppose they could have gone off the road and I zoomed past not seeing them. It was worth a try.

I flagged down a car coming from the direction I had just ridden.

"Yeah, I saw some great big thing – wasn't exactly sure what it was," he replied. "But I did notice a man and two kids sitting on the side of the road about three miles back."

What the heck? Was it some kind of magic trick? Had they disappeared, only to reappear after I had already passed? I sent a message back with another motorist.

"Where were you?" John shouted when he finally approached the gas station in Humptulips. "We sat by the side of the road waiting for ages! We went really slowly and finally stopped altogether. We were afraid you had trouble with your bike or had gotten sick or something!"

We continued on our way, pondering the mystery of somehow missing each other on that narrow strip of shoulder on the side of the road.

"I got it!" I shouted some twenty minutes later. "Way back at the campground – when you were first heading out to the highway – did you go right or left?"

John looked at me like I was nuts. "I went back the same way we came in."

"That's it! That's where it all happened!" I explained. "There was a 'Y' back there – just a few hundred feet from the campsite. It said to go left for Highway 101 South, so I went left. But yesterday we came from the north so came in on the other branch of the Y. I bet that's where it happened – I got ahead of you in the first couple minutes of the day!"

The mystery of ships passing in the middle of the night was solved.

It wasn't long before John and I became obsessed with making miles. Maybe that was because we hadn't made any for so long – the Oregon coast just wouldn't let us go. After those first few weeks where we cycled like mad, our pace had slowed to a creep.

It seemed like each and every time we started pedaling something popped up to demand that we stop. We climbed sand dunes, played on beaches, and toured cheese factories. We hiked to the top of mountains and picked blackberries by the water bottleful. It was life in the slow lane – the *very* slow lane. After ten twenty-mile days along the coast, John and I decided we need to pick up the pace. Sure, we were out to play and have fun, but we also wanted to see more that year than just the Oregon coast.

We were cruising along and saw a sign: *Yaquina Lighthouse*

"Wanna go see a lighthouse, Nancy?" John called back to me as I pedaled behind him.

I made a split-second decision and called back. "Nah. Let's skip it. We've seen enough lighthouses."

"I wanna go!" whined Daryl.

"Me too!" added Davy.

Dear Grandma,

This is the 42nd day of the trip. I had a running race with Dad to the outhouse in the campground. We made an explosion by pouring stove fuel on paper and lighting it on fire. Mommy passed us on the road today and we didn't know it. We thought she was in trouble. We found her later. We rode in the rain and got soaked.

Love, Davy

No amount of coaxing or cajoling could talk them out of it. We turned the corner and headed toward the coastline. As it turned out, that road to the lighthouse was like the yellow brick road taking us to incredible and extraordinary places. The Land of Oz couldn't hold a candle to that area, no matter how incredible it might be. The old lighthouse we thought we were going to visit was pretty neat indeed, but the rocks it warned of were even better.

We were entertained for hours by sea stars, sea urchins, and other marine life in tide pools.

"Look!" the kids shouted as they climbed down the rock face to the tide pools. John and I gathered with the boys as we marveled at a dozen starfish clinging to a rock face.

A second later the kids were off and running. "Mom! Come over here! These are really cool!" I clamored over more rocks until I stood by my boys gazing at an underwater fantasy land filled with sea anemones blooming like bizarre underwater flowers.

"Ooh – these look nasty!" Daryl exclaimed when they found a patch of sea urchins with needlelike spines threatening to pierce their shoes should they fall in.

From rock to rock the kids leaped, discovering more treasures in each tide pool. Each rock revealed its own mysteries – special formations or sea creatures my boys had never seen before.

All too soon, the tide began to come in and we were forced off the rocks. Somewhere I could almost hear Dorothy clicking her heels, wanting to go home. But I didn't want to leave my own personal Land of Oz.

Dear Granda,

We went to a lighthouse. It was fun. I saw a sea anemone, sea urchin, sunflower sea star, starfish, and a big red sea urchin. We touched the inside of a sea anemone. It was sticky and closed its mouth. The sunflower sea star had twenty four legs! All of the sea urchins were purple except the red one. Sea anemones are green. The sea urchins had sharp spines. I found almost all the cool stuff. Two boys fell in the water. I bet they were cold and hurt. My foot fell in the water. It was cold.

Love, Daryl

Slowly we made our way toward the California border. Oregon was wonderful, but we were excited about all California had to offer. Exactly two months after we pulled out of our driveway we crossed into our fourth state. The boys were giddy with excitement at the thought that they made it – they had pedaled well over a thousand miles and had entered California at last. I couldn't wait to explore the redwoods and the wonderful state parks California is known for. I went to bed with a smile on my face – we had arrived.

Rerouted for Love

What was it the Byrds sang about? *To everything (turn, turn turn)... There is a season (turn, turn, turn)... And a time for every purpose under heaven...*

There comes a time for everything. A time to be a wife. A time to be a mother. And a time to be a daughter. After two months on the road, the time came for me to leave my husband and sons to be a daughter. My mother called and I needed to go home.

Just a few days before we departed on our journey, my mother had been diagnosed with cancer. We batted all possibilities around – cancel the trip, postpone it, go anyway. In the end, we opted for the latter, knowing the time might come when one or more of us would be needed at home. That time came just after we crossed the border into California, and I rented a car to drive to Boise.

John spent the day reorganizing and repacking, trying to fit everything on one bike. All that gear – that mountain of equipment – needed to be stashed, buckled or tied onto the triple. Everything he could possibly ditch was put in the rental car. The four of us quietly hung around the hotel room, putting off the moment of departure. We knew it would be tough. I wanted more than anything to be with them. And yet, I needed to be home with Mom. If only... if only I could figure out a way to do it all. But I knew, and John knew, and the kids knew, that just wasn't possible.

"We promise to take care of Daddy," the kids told me. "We'll help him a lot!"

"Take care of my boys," I pleaded John. "I'll miss you so."

And with that, I started the car and drove away, leaving a part of my heart behind.

The first few days of their male bonding time was spent cycling through the mighty redwoods. Their bike, as massive as it was, seemed small and insignificant in comparison to the gigantic trees towering on either side of the road. As my boys (all three of them) made their way into the fog-shrouded depths of the redwood forest, 300-foot-tall trees towered above them on either side of the road and, as large as it was, their bike was dwarfed by the magnificence of the trees.

"You should've seen it, Mom!" Davy told me one evening on the telephone. "We hiked to Corkscrew Tree today! It's a great big redwood tree that's all twisted and mangled. It was so cool! And we also hiked to see Big Tree. That's a really old tree. They say it's 1500 years old! And it is 304 feet tall – can you imagine that? It's huge!"

"But that's not the best part, Mom," added Daryl. "We also rode through the Yurok Reservation and they were having a salmon festival. Daddy bought us a great big chunk of salmon that was roasting over the fire right by the side of the road. It was so good!"

Daryl enjoyed smoked salmon at the salmon festival on the Yurok Reservation.

I sat at home in Idaho, wishing I could be on the California coast with my husband and children. I remembered visiting northern California as a child and seeing the enormous redwood trees and precipitous cliffs along Highway 1. Those images stayed with me my whole life, and I couldn't wait to take my own children there. Instead, I was relegated to hearing their tales over the phone line and seeing their photos on the internet. It wasn't the same, but I could feel the excitement in the boys' voices as they proclaimed their wonder at some of the very sights I remembered so vividly from my own childhood. I felt like I could almost get a glimpse of the redwood forest and spectacular ocean views through my children's eyes.

The boys were having the time of their life. Every day brought new adventures, and Mother Nature was at her best. One morning they were trapped in their campsite by a group of elk on the road. Unable to pass by, they simply sat on the side of the road admiring the magnificent animals until the path was clear. They took advantage of the Redwoods National Park's Junior Ranger program to learn about banana slugs. They discovered many state parks where they found water holes and spent delightful hours swimming and playing. In short, they had discovered heaven.

Mom and I kept up with their adventures through our online journal and evening phone calls. Mom had suffered a terrible reaction to her chemotherapy and nearly died, but was now recovering and gaining strength. We enjoyed following along with the boys as they traveled.

As the trio worked their way south along the coast they took advantage of the many state parks California had to offer.

"Hey, Mom!" Daryl chattered excitedly into the telephone. "We're at MacKerricher State Park – and this place is wonderful! There are so many places to play. Today we played in the tide pools. I stuck my finger in a sea anemone and it closed up around it – it was really gooshy!"

"Tomorrow we'll climb some sand dunes and play on the beach and take a hike into the forest. We're having a lot of fun, Mom!" Davy added.

The boys were fascinated by the stunted trees in the pygmy forest. They were stunted due to the unique physical conditions in the area.

A few days later the boys went hiking in the Pygmy Forest in Van Damme State Park. They marveled at the mature, cone-bearing cypress and pine trees which stood anywhere from six inches to eight feet tall.

"Do you know how the Pygmy Forest happened, Mom?" the boys asked me that night. I admitted that not only did I not know how it happened, I had never even heard of its existence.

"We took a long hike out in the Pygmy Forest and learned a lot about it. And we got lost, so we spent more time there than we had planned, but it's a really interesting place. They said the trees are stunted because there's something about the water under the ground and strange soils that don't let the trees grow like normal. The trees are tiny, but they are really old. They say they can be hundreds of years old!"

In the mornings my boys were enveloped in thick fog as they pedaled along sheer cliffs high over the Pacific Ocean. By late mornings, the sun had burned the fog away and the three adventurers were rewarded with spectacular views of the sparkling waters far below them.

Those spectacular views, however, came at a price. As the highway snaked its way along the coastline it climbed thousands of feet toward the heavens only to plummet back down again. The boys ground up massive hill after massive hill, becoming more and more weary.

The constant climbing and descending along the California coast exhausted us.

"I'm exhausted," John told me one night on the phone. "We just now arrived into a campground. I haven't cooked dinner yet, nor set up the tent. We just pulled in – it took us all day to

pedal a mere forty miles. All that extra weight on the bike really makes a difference. I don't know if I can do this, Nance. I'm wiped out."

Dear Mommy and Grandma,

Do you know why redwoods are called redwoods? It is because they have red wood. When I look at them they are grey, but when you break off the bark it is red. This is because the outside gets weathered. We went swimming in a swimming hole. It is getting hot because we are going away from the ocean.

Love, Daryl

Dear Mommy and Grandma,

We went on a hike in the pygmy forest. We turned the wrong direction and had to walk a long way until we found that out. Daryl and Daddy had a big pine cone fight. I was the judge. It was a tie. Today we were along the coast and there was a huge cliff by the side of the road. It was so dangerous that everyone was scared.

Love, Davy

Within a couple weeks the group had settled into a rhythm. It took John ninety minutes every morning to get the boys up and fed, the tent stowed, and the bike packed. Riding all day was tough, but they slowed down their daily mileage and took advantage of other activities the California coast had for them.

My mom and I also settled into a routine – a routine that consisted of doctor's appointments and waiting for phone calls from John. We checked the online journal every hour, hoping for an update. Although all was going well with the boys, we both knew we were pushing our luck. One adult with two boys alone on the road was a situation asking for trouble.

And trouble came the day they pulled into Santa Cruz.

"You wouldn't believe what happened yesterday," John complained on the phone the next morning. "We were doing really well – we knocked off sixty miles quick and easy with an unbelievable tailwind! We figured we were in for a great evening hanging out around the campfire."

"But then everything changed. We were only six miles from the campground, but ended up with a flat tire. You know how it is, Nancy. The rear tire on the triple is such a pain to fix, so I decided to just pump it up and try to make it to the campground. But then I noticed the tarp was gone – it had fallen off the trailer."

I sat there listening, laughing at his frustration. My mom watched me, wondering what the conversation was about.

"I sent the kids back along the road to see if they could find the tarp," he continued. "I told them to walk back a ways, and if it wasn't there to come back. I filled the tire and started riding back to find them."

"A short while later, the tire went flat again. It was starting to get dark and I was getting worried about the kids. I never thought they would go that far! I parked the bike in someone's yard and took off running after the kids."

My laughter stopped and I listened to the rest of his tale. I knew something had to happen. I just wasn't sure what that something was.

"So anyway, Mom," I relayed the tale to my mother. "John was panicking by this time. The kids were nowhere to be seen. They were in a strange California city and wandering the streets alone. John was getting frantic."

"He approached a man walking along the street. 'Have you seen two kids in orange shirts?' The man had no idea what he was talking about."

"John kept running in the direction he had sent the kids," I explained. "Eventually a couple walking along the road said they had seen them a little while before. John took off at high speed. By that time, it was pitch black and he had no idea how much farther ahead they were. A mile or so later, he finally caught up to them." Mom breathed a sigh of relief.

"Once they got back to the bike, John tried pumping up the tire again, but it wouldn't hold air at all. He took the whole thing apart under a streetlight and fixed the tube. Mom, you have no idea how much of a hassle it is to fix that thing. You have to take the trailer off and disconnect the disc brake. Then you can take the tire off and repair it before putting the whole thing together again. It usually takes both of us to get it fixed, but now it's only him – the boys just aren't coordinated enough or strong enough to do a whole lot."

"The upshot of all this is that they didn't get to the campground until 10:06 p.m. last night. All three of them were exhausted and famished. John set up the tent while the kids munched on granola bars. I guess it really isn't all that bad – they made it, after all. They are all fine. Exhausted, but alive and well."

Mom and I knew we had to do something.

"Nancy," Mom told me later that day. "You need to be there with the boys. I worry about them so much anyway, and after hearing what happened yesterday I'm even more worried. If you had been there, the boys would not have had to walk back alone. You need to be there."

"I will Mom," I replied. "Glenda is coming in a week. Once she's here, I'll head back."

"No. You need to go now. It's too dangerous. John shouldn't be there alone with those kids. They've been on their own for a month already and have tempted fate too long. Too much can happen. I'm okay now. I'm still a bit weak, but I can get around. If you make sure I have enough food for a week, I'll be fine until your sister gets here. I've got good neighbors in case I need anything. Seriously, I think you should go. Now.

A couple days later I arrived in Monterey, returned the rental car, jumped on my trusty steed, and set out along the beautiful California coast to Big Sur, where my family was camped awaiting me. Turquoise waters... stunning cliffs... and a strong tailwind. What more could I ask for? As much as I would have loved to take my time, I didn't take any breaks at all because I was giddy with excitement about getting back to my boys and I needed to make sure I was at the campground by dark.

I pulled into the town of Big Sur about an hour before dark and patted myself on my back in congratulations. I smugly called Mom and announced that I had done it! I had pulled it off! Yes! (Insert image of me pumping my fist in victory at this point.) I figured I only had three miles to go and I still had an hour or so of daylight. Yes, I had made it. I had gone from Boise to Big Sur in one mighty leap!

I climbed back on my bike and started pedaling through the forest toward the campground. I pedaled and pedaled and was sure that the campground was just around the next corner... maybe the next... And then suddenly I broke out of the valley and saw a lake on my left. A big lake. I thought, *Hmm... it seems strange that there would be a lake that big right next to the ocean.*

Then I noticed the sun setting over the lake, and it dawned on me that there was no lake over on my left. That was a pond. *The* pond. The Pacific pond. I had learned a thing or two in my forty-six years on this planet and one of them was that if you are pedaling south along the California coast, the ocean will be on your right. But that ocean was very definitely on my left.

That's when my hand came up and smacked myself upside the head and I realized that I had done something really stupid. That moment when I got turned around at the store and headed back north was most definitely one of those moments of absolute, complete, total, unutterable dumbness.

I turned around and pedaled for all I was worth back toward the valley and the forest. At that point I did not have only three miles to go and an hour of daylight. Now I had over five miles to go, and the sun was setting over the ocean. I pedaled as hard as I could along the twisty, winding road through the forest and realized that I had absolutely no lights on my bike whatsoever; no way to alert oncoming drivers that I was there. Those visions of a grand reunion that I had been having all day turned into something not quite so grand; something involving images of my beloved kids scraping my guts off the highway.

One way or another, I arrived at the campground without incident, relieved that my kids wouldn't have to deal with the grisly scene of my imagination. I fell asleep with my boys tucked up on either side of me and marveled at how wonderful it was to be back "home" in our tent once more.

Culinary Pursuits

After fifteen hundred miles along the coast, we turned left and headed inland. The lure of the Grand Canyon was too strong to resist, even if it meant a thousand mile detour to get there. We had climbed plenty of hills along the coast, but they ended up being nothing more than ant hills compared to what California threw at us as we headed east.

Range after massive range blocked our path, and we climbed up thousands of feet only to plunge down the other side. But that wasn't the hardest part. We had left the coast – the bicycling mecca of North America. Gone were the daily campgrounds and showers. Gone were the stores every few miles. Gone were the detailed bicycling maps telling us exactly what we would face on any given day. All we had was an AAA map which more or less showed us the way. We learned quickly to stock up on food and water each and every chance we got. We sought out national forests and other unoccupied lands for our tent at night. Life was an adventure once again.

Distances between towns became enormous after we left the coast. Those distances threw us a few logistical challenges as we tried to figure out how much food and water we would need.

All went well for the first week or so away from the coast. The scenery was spectacular and the people were wonderful. We were in biker's no man's land where few cyclists ever passed. We aroused a lot of curiosity and attracted more attention than we wanted.

Eventually we arrived into Bakersfield where we stayed with newfound friends. We asked them about a route out of the city.

"There really isn't a good way out," Michael said. "You'll have to go over the mountains if you want to go east – there's only one road going in that direction. You could go south, but that won't get you to the Grand Canyon."

We decided to attack the mountains head-on and continued pedaling eastward. Until we arrived at a gas station, that is.

"Oh my lord! You can't!" cried a woman filling her gas tank when we stopped to ask directions. "You just can't! You'll be killed if you try to ride The Canyon!"

All the other motorists standing around joined in. "The Canyon is a death trap!" "It's narrow and twisty and windy. Not a place for cyclists." "Go another way – please!"

They had just managed to screw up our day even more. As if it wasn't bad enough that we had taken a wrong turn and climbed the *wrong* very steep hill, now we had to revamp our entire plan. If we didn't go through The Canyon, well... we would have to change plans entirely.

We turned around and screamed back down the hill, climbed up the right one, and arrived into the campsite just as the last vestiges of daylight were disappearing. We knew decision time had come. We either had to face certain death in The Canyon on the morrow, or turn around and go back to the coast.

"Holy dooley! Look at all this! Where are you folks headed on that contraption?"

John and I looked up to see a young man walking into our campsite. "It looks like we've come to the end of our road," John sighed. "We've pedaled all the way from Boise, but now we've been told we can't cycle The Canyon. Unfortunately, there really isn't any option if we want to go to Death Valley and the Grand Canyon."

"Who said that?" questioned Steve, the local bike activist who had barged into our campsite. "Listen guys – you can do it. I've done it plenty of times. You've got to understand Bakersfield – the people here don't ride bikes. Sure – they have a great bike path through the city, but you could probably count the serious cyclists on one hand. Now don't get me wrong – I don't have anything against the local people. After all, I am one. But here's the reality – Bakersfield just doesn't have a real "bike culture" going on. We're trying – our little handful of serious cyclists – we're trying to change things, but it's a long, slow process."

"If you've managed to pedal that thing 3000 miles, you can pedal The Canyon," Steve continued. "It won't be the most pleasant experience of your trip, but it's doable. I've done it many times. Just do it. It's not that bad."

John and I fell asleep that night wondering just how bad the ride through The Canyon would be.

I never thought road construction could be such a godsend, but some people figure it saved our lives that day. As we approached the mouth of The Canyon, we rode past an enormous line of waiting cars. For what seemed like miles, cars sat idle as drivers and passengers chatted or read. People milled about on the side of the road, in and out of cars, waiting, as we pedaled by.

Anxiety grew as we drew nearer the mouth of the canyon. Was it really as dangerous as people had warned? Would we be obliterated on the first curve? Or not until near the top? Or could it possibly be a piece of cake? We tenuously pedaled past car after car, wondering which one would do the deed. In time we passed a construction site at the mouth of the canyon and headed in.

The canyon was narrow, the road twisty, and a shoulder nonexistent. Flaggers had just released a long stream of vehicles, and they whizzed past us one after the other. We pulled over and waited for them all to pass. Once the massive backlog of cars had passed we had the road to ourselves. Rather than being the horrible experience some had told us it would be, riding The Canyon was quite nice. A beautiful deep canyon with a rushing river on one side of the road and a massive cliff face on the other. Knowing that all the cars were stopped at the construction site below, we relaxed and enjoyed the ride.

Thirty minutes later we saw another stream of vehicles in our rear view mirrors and pulled over to let the caravan pass.

The Canyon, far from being the death-defying, bicyclist-smashing canyon from hell, ended up being a great ride. Every twenty or thirty minutes another stream of cars came by and we pulled over to take a break. Once the road was clear, we headed merrily on our way, knowing we had the road to ourselves for at least another twenty minutes.

Eventually we reached the end of the canyon and continued on through flatlands. Night was nigh and we needed a spot to pitch our tent – after we filled our water bottles at the next store. But the store didn't exist. No, I guess I shouldn't say that – it existed, but it had been closed for the past thirteen years according to the good folk on the porch of a neighboring house.

"Heck yeah, you can have some water!" they shouted in response to our question. "And if you wait a few minutes you can have some steak too!" We collapsed onto Jerry and Barb's porch to wait for steak. "You guys came up from Bakersfield today? You rode The Canyon? Are you nuts?"

"I suppose you could say that. But we're having a blast anyway!"

"We bagged a buck today! We'd been tracking him for a week – and today we got the sucker. We're celebrating tonight, baby! Steak and sausages for us!" Jerry lit a rousing fire in the grill. "Just wait. You've got a treat coming! I cook the best steak in the county!"

Jerry was right. He cooked up the best steak I had eaten in a long time and we enjoyed our evening with our newfound friends. We also enjoyed camping on their living room floor as well.

Meeting and getting to know people like Jerry and Barb was a highlight of our journey.

> *Dear Grandma*
>
> *I probably shouldn't tell you what I did, but it was so much fun and the kids learned so much that I'm going to anyway. For the first time on the trip we passed a rattlesnake sleeping along the road, and I figured I couldn't miss the opportunity to 'educate' the kids about what a real rattler sounds like. I got the flagpole off the trailer and had the kids stand way back as I poked the snake. It didn't do anything until I actually touched it, then it rattled like you wouldn't believe as it slithered away. Now the kids know what to listen for anyway. I'm hoping that will keep them safe if we ever find another one.*
>
> *Love, John*

We headed out early from Jerry and Barb's house with full intentions of making it over a nearby pass in the cool of the morning. Fate, however, had other plans.

Ten miles from the house I was following closely behind John when I heard, "Pssss!" and was showered with some kind of liquid. A second later it came again – "Pssss" and a quick dowsing of liquid. I soon realized it was coming from John's bike and each revolution of the tire brought a "Pssss" and another shower.

"John! Stop!" I shouted. "Your tire is spitting goop!"

John took one look at his tire and realized it was completely worn down – to the point where he had an actual hole worn in it. As the air escaped it had taken the bright green puncture-sealing goop with it.

"How in the heck did that happen?" I asked. "I've been seeing you diligently check your tires every day."

"I know," John replied. "I'm baffled. The last time my tires wore out, it was the front one that went. I just figured the triple has a totally different wear pattern than most bikes, so have been checking my front tire every day. I didn't even think to look at the rear one. In any case, this thing is shot. It's trashed. I need a new tire."

The problem was that we were in the middle of nowhere – quite literally. We were stuck seventy-five miles from Bakersfield, but that was the closest place a tire might be available. This was not good. We put on our thinking caps to figure out how we could snare a tire.

"Nancy! I've got it!" John blurted. "Jerry mentioned he was leaving around ten to go to Bakersfield! It's 9:40 now. Go! Hurry! Get back to Jerry's house and you can ride into town with him!"

I frantically flagged down the first passing car and begged them to take me back. They looked at me blankly, and mumbled something to each other in Spanish. I switched gears. "*¡Tengo que ir a la casa de un amigo! ¡Alli!*" They nodded their heads, although their eyes betrayed their confusion. Jerry was just climbing in the truck when I barged into the yard.

In Bakersfield I bought a tire, went out to a Mexican restaurant for lunch with Jerry and Barb (I will admit I felt a bit guilty knowing the boys were sweltering in the hot sun while I was indulging, but certainly not too guilty!) before heading out for the ninety-minute journey to find them.

Jerry and I found John and the boys seeking shade beneath a large joshua tree, and we were fixing the tire when a police car pulled up.

"Do you know what the story about these bikes is?" the policeman asked. "I got a call that there were some bicycles here, and that pretty much freaked out the old folk around here."

We explained our predicament, and let him know we would be back on the road in a few minutes.

"Can't say as how I blame those people," he said. "Round here, only poor folk who can't afford cars ride bikes. Those old folks – they saw those bikes parked in front of this house and couldn't figure out what was going on. They knew this here house is empty – the owners are on vacation. It sure seemed mighty strange to have these bikes parked here in front of the house all day, and they figured that maybe you all were breaking in to the house."

I just shook my head and wondered just how those old folks expected us to carry away all those belongings they feared we were stealing.

As we made our way eastward the mountains grew steadily bigger and the passes higher. We thought back to our days on the coast with thousand-foot climbs and wondered just how we thought they were so difficult. Our daily routine now regularly included climbing two- or three-thousand-foot passes, and then plummeting back down the other side. Days were hot, but about to get even hotter.

As we neared Death Valley, we knew we were in for a challenge. The Panamint Range stood before us, hiding the wonders of the lowest point in North America. In order to get there, however, we would have to cross our highest pass yet – Emigrant Pass at 5318 feet above sea level. Given the fact that we were starting out below sea level, it was one hell of a climb.

The boys walked up steep hills as it was easier for John to pedal solo.

Stashing as much water as possible into our panniers, we set off for the sixty-mile trek to the next water source 4200 vertical feet higher than where we started. The first few miles weren't bad, but eventually the climb started and the going got tough. Cars were few and far between as we slowly ground our way up through a narrow canyon. The kids had long since gotten off the bike to walk, leaving John alone on the triple. I walked my bike alongside the boys. All four of us were drenched in sweat and thirsty beyond belief, knowing we had to preserve our precious water.

And then those Road Angels entered the picture again. Each and every one of the few cars who passed stopped to offer water. Or orange juice. Or candy bars. By the time we reached the campground, we were carrying the same amount of water we had started the day with even after spending the whole day climbing.

"I don't like this," John said as he glanced around the campground and at the darkening sky. "A storm is moving in and this campground is totally exposed. If the storm brings high winds, our tent won't be able to handle it." He set off to see what he could round up.

As the kids and I waited, the storm drew closer. Lightning flashed and the seconds between the flash and the deafening roar of thunder decreased rapidly. Wind kicked up large clouds of dust from the campground floor.

"I found a place!" John yelled as he raced toward us. "Grab your bike and come with me!" By now the rain had started and was coming down in drops that felt like large rats when they smashed into our arms and legs.

"It's just up there! We're almost there!"

Fortunately, John had found a ranger who gave him permission to set up camp in a storage shed belonging to the national parks. It was a very basic structure closed on three sides but open to the elements on the fourth. For us, it was perfect. It was a roof over our heads and we slept well listening to rain pelt the corrugated tin roof all night.

The following morning the four of us crested the pass and plunged down the other side. We felt the air steadily increasing in temperature as we screamed down into the valley. We descended lower and lower and felt heat waves radiating out of the ground – as though the flames of hell were escaping.

By the time we arrived at the campground two hundred feet below sea level, the wind was scalding hot and it felt as though we were standing in front of a huge, blazing fire with tongues of flame worming their way into our throats. We collapsed onto some campground benches and wondered just how we were ever going to get out of this one. Sure, the climb to get into the valley was tough – but the climb out would be even harder. And in this blazing heat, I wasn't sure we were up to the task.

The following day we stayed put. It was 107 degrees – cool, we had been told. We had intended to cycle to the lowest point in North America, but it was just too hot. We spent the day in the air-conditioned national park visitor's center and learned more than we thought there was to know about the valley.

Death Valley

That evening we sat around our campsite pondering how we could get out of the valley. Our only hope was to leave early – very early – and get as many miles in as possible before it heated up. John convinced me to pack the tent and sleep under the stars in order to speed up packing the next morning. I hate sleeping under the stars.

As romantic as it sounds, I just don't sleep when I'm not safely ensconced in my nylon home. The wind blows my hair and tickles my body and I just can't sleep. Before I crawled into bed, I made sure my hair was braided tightly to keep it pulled back, but it didn't take long for a few little wisps to escape from their braids and start to tickle my cheeks.

I pushed the hairs back and flipped over. They jumped back out. I pushed them back.

I got up and rummaged through my panniers until I found my bandanna and wrapped that around my head – that should hold my hair in place. It worked for a few minutes, but eventually the wind managed to pull a few wisps of hair out again.

By now I was desperate. I. Needed. Sleep. We would be getting up before dawn to climb out of the valley. It would be a massive 3400-foot climb and was sure to be hot. I needed to sleep.

John and the boys slept peacefully beside me while I wracked my brain to solve my dilemma. Finally I crawled completely under my sleeping bag – that should block the wind! That lasted all of a minute before I sheepishly crawled back out covered in sweat. That obviously wasn't a good solution to my problem.

I built my sleeping bag up into a wind-breaking barrier and hunkered down behind it. That lasted a few seconds before my barrier crashed down in a heap of nylon and feathers.

I finally pulled out my spare t-shirt and wrapped my entire head, leaving only a small hole for my nose and mouth. That worked. I drifted off to Dreamland.

"Nancy! Nancy!" John called a few minutes later. "Nancy!" He called with an urgency typically reserved for an emergency. The last time he used that tone of voice was when a skunk was pillaging our food stash immediately outside the tent. I sat up in a panic, sure that some kind of famished predator was lurking nearby – and this time we didn't even have the protective walls of the tent surrounding us. "Do you know where the oatmeal is?"

I mumbled something about stashing it in my pannier and lay back down to sleep.

And then those hairs crept out and started dancing on my face again.

I looked over at John, who was peacefully sleeping now that he knew where the oatmeal was. Why was it so important to find out now, in the middle of the night, where the oatmeal was? What was so bloody important about that oatmeal that he needed to wake me up in the wee hours of the morning to find out where it was? He interrupted my hard-earned sleep to ask about OATMEAL? What an inconsiderate slob he must be to deprive me of a few hours of sleep like that! How could he even think of doing such an incredibly self-centered, egomaniacal thing? Doesn't he care about my sleep? *I'll be climbing 3400 feet out of this god-forsaken valley in the morning, and now I'll be a total zombie – thanks to that ungrateful sod!*

I looked again at that man lying there in blissful sleep, with the wind gently caressing him into dreamland and realized how easy it would be to get rid of him. But then I looked at my little angels curled beside him and realized that they needed someone to haul them out of the valley on the morrow. Besides, it was too blasted hot to dig a hole for a body.

I rolled over and went back to sleep.

As we heated up water for breakfast in the morning, I asked John about the oatmeal.

"I heard coyotes singing last night," he told me, "and I wondered if they were eating my Strawberries and Cream breakfast. I actually climbed out of bed and looked for it, but couldn't find it on the table. I couldn't bear the thought that I might not get my oatmeal this morning."

I simply shook my head and ate my Blueberries and Cream oatmeal in silence.

To our surprise, the climb out of Death Valley was tough, but not overly obnoxious. Shortly thereafter, however, we noticed a change. Maybe it was our reaction to the heat and arduous climbs we had endured lately, or perhaps it was just a natural reaction to being on the road for four months, but we had turned into a bunch of wacky sarcastic bitches either laughing hysterically or bickering endlessly. One day it all came to a head.

We hit a new low in our culinary pursuits that morning. We had eaten peanut butter and jelly for breakfast many times throughout our journey. PB & J sandwiches, PB & J on tortillas, PB & J on crackers... But that morning we had only PB & J. By the spoonful. But as John so gallantly pointed out, at least we had a choice. I had a whole pannier full of food – rice, spaghetti, soup – but it all required cooking, and we didn't feel like cooking. So we ate peanut butter and jelly instead, which may not have been the most nutritionally sound meal we ever ate, but wasn't the worst either.

I had learned over the years to leave the task of taking the tent down to John. John was, in a word, *fastidious* about the tent. It needed to be folded *just so*, with every part in its place. Invariably I messed it up by my very presence. Normally I busied myself with other chores while John prepared the tent, but that morning I had nothing to pack since we had never unpacked the previous night. Against my better judgment, I headed over to help my husband with the tent.

As I arrived, John picked up the tent and asked me to shake off the tarp we used as a ground cloth to protect the tent floor. We had slept in sand that night and there was a fair amount of it on the tarp. I gently shook the sand off in the wind and laid the tarp back down. I managed to get it fairly flat, but there was a slight wrinkle on the opposite side. "Would you put your foot on that corner so it doesn't blow away while I get this flat?" I asked John as he stood with an armful of nylon.

The next thing I knew John had shoved the tent in my arms and snatched the tarp off the ground. "I'll do it!" he grunted. "I don't know why you can't do it right – it isn't that hard!" He shook the tarp violently in the wind to get rid of the last few grains of invisible sand, and flung it down on the ground. He looked up at me with a smile of smug satisfaction. "See – it isn't that hard. Why couldn't you do that?" He let go of the tarp and rose to get the tent from my arms. The wind caught the tarp and folded it neatly in half.

John paused for a second, then casually walked to the bikes and grabbed a few stakes. He put a stake in one corner of the tarp and moved to Corner B. Corner A pulled out of the ground and began waving wildly in the wind like a whip. I silently snickered to myself.

John calmly picked up the tarp and stakes and moved to a different section of the ground where the surface wasn't quite so sandy. He had pinned A down and started on B when A broke free and flapped wildly in the wind once again. I broke out into a full-fledged giggle, and John shot me a look that could kill.

John managed to get a stake in Corner A and held his foot on it while he did a sort of deep lunge toward Corner B. By that time my giggles had changed to howls of laughter and the front side of the tarp flapped up and entangled itself around John's head and arms. John continued calmly playing some kind of bizarre game of Twister as the wind fought him, while I laughed hysterically and patiently held the tent until he needed it.

In time, John managed to get the tarp staked down and the tent put away and I was quite certain there was neither one grain of sand nor wrinkled piece of nylon in the bag.

All this time, the kids were bickering. A lot. (I wondered if it might have had something to do with our 'nutritious' breakfast?) I packed up my bike listening to the kids fight about who got a particular rock or quarrel about whose hiding place the crawl space under a bush was. John and I rounded the boys up and herded them onto the bike as they squabbled and argued about anything and everything.

Finally, we were able to get them to agree on one thing: to sing. As we fought a headwind, they sang, "Jingle bells, Batman smells... Robin laid an egg. Batmobile, lost a wheel..." That worked for a while until Davy got tired of it and stopped singing. Daryl continued... which annoyed Davy... and Davy turned around to smack his brother and yell at him to shut up. Daryl stopped.

He stopped until Davy started singing again... and they both sang until Davy tired of it and stopped... and Daryl continued... and Davy turned around and smacked him and yelled at him to stop.

Now it just so happened that John had a splitting headache and was quickly tiring of fighting the hill and the headwind, which meant he wasn't all that eager to listen to a couple of kids fighting and arguing over a whole lot of nothing. And every time Davy turned around to smack his brother, the whole triple bike lurched like a drunken sailor.

Finally John had had enough and he slammed on the brakes. I happened to be following immediately behind him and couldn't stop quickly enough. I smacked into the trailer and tumbled down to the pavement.

"Get off!" John shouted at Davy. "Get off right now! I mean it!"

Davy climbed off the bike in silence while I picked myself off the pavement. John took off with Daryl still attached to the bike, leaving me and Davy to fend for ourselves. I rode slowly for a mile or so with Davy jogging alongside me until John had cooled off enough to allow his son back on the bike.

We continued climbing a major hill against a headwind in complete silence. John was pumping as hard as he could, but the hill was steeper than it looked and he was tired. "Pedal harder!"

John shouted at the boys. Davy and Daryl dug deep and pedaled as hard as they could. All four of us were panting and sweating, with no end in sight, when a car pulled up beside us.

"Hey! Remember us?" A couple emerged from the car and came toward us as we stood straddling our bikes. "We met you at the campground in Death Valley."

We chatted with them for a few minutes before they headed toward their car to take off. "Say," they said as they walked away. "You want us to take the kids up to the top?"

"Yeah!" the boys shouted as they made a beeline for the car.

"We'll meet you at the top of the hill," the couple informed us as they pulled away, leaving John and me standing, childless, on the side of the road.

"What have we just done?" John asked. "We just sent our kids off with complete strangers! What if we never see them again?"

The two of us panicked and raced up the pass in search of our precious boys. Fortunately, the car was waiting for us at the top and the boys were just fine. We made a mental note that we needed to be a bit more careful and a bit less trusting. All those Road Angels we were meeting were turning us into something we didn't quite recognize.

You know those signs that warn of animals on the road? Generally they have a picture of a deer jumping out in the road. As we cycled through the Nevada desert, we saw something like a deer sign, but this one had a picture of a turtle. I tried looking at the sign in every conceivable manner to figure out what animal it could possibly be, but it was most definitely a turtle.

There aren't turtles out here in the middle of the desert, I thought. I came to the conclusion that the sign was some kind of joke. It wasn't.

We helped Mr. Turtle off the road into the safety of the bushes.

We were merrily pedaling along looking for a campsite in the desert when we found him – Mr. Turtle. He was sitting in the middle of the road waiting for a truck to smash him to smithereens. The boys gently picked him up and delivered him to the sage brush on the side of the road. I like to think we did our good deed for the day – we saved Mr. Turtle from certain demise.

A few days later, there was no sign. We were screaming down a hill when John suddenly slammed on the brakes. Fortunately I was following far enough behind that I could stop, so I pulled up behind him.

"Get the camera! Get the camera!" John was shouting. "Get off the bike! Did you see him?" I looked around – totally bewildered. The only thing I saw was a gigantic semi-truck quickly bearing down upon us. "Go back, Nance! He's back there! Turn around and go back!"

I figured my husband had finally lost it for good, but I dutifully turned my bike around and headed back – just what I was headed for was anyone's guess. Eventually I found him – Mr. Tarantula. Sitting in the middle of the road. The big truck zoomed past – and swung wide to avoid us. He missed our newfound friend by a few inches.

The boys and I gawked for a while – it was the first wild tarantula we had seen – then we gently coaxed our friend into the sage brush and said goodbye. We like to think that Mr. Tarantula met Mr. Turtle and compared notes about their good Samaritans.

Jack Frost and Carrot Soup

As we pedaled toward the Grand Canyon, fall was in the air and Mother Nature played even more spectacular cards than we could have dreamed of. Day after day we cycled through new and unique territory with fascinating rock formations and brilliant colors. Trees, when we found them, were at the height of beauty with reds, yellows, and oranges contrasting with the surrounding rock formations.

When we arrived at Lake Mead Recreation Area we were awed by mile upon mile of spectacular desert scenery. Huge patches of red Aztec sandstone mixed haphazardly with incredible rock formations to make a kind of giant playland. It looked as though a baby giant had toddled through the canyons with a giant-sized red crayon, coloring splotches here and there, willy-nilly, with no apparent rhyme or reason as to their placement.

Camping out was wonderful and the kids had a great time exploring enormous sandstone hills. They climbed over and around them discovering interesting formations and caves formed by erosion. The early morning sun brought out colors in a spectacular manner and we were spellbound by the beauty of reds emanating from the Aztec sandstone in the area as we watched our breath freeze into little clouds in front of our mouths.

Ideal biking conditions always seem to be short-lived, and this was one of those times. Due to some engineer's poor decision-making skills, there was no option besides the interstate if one wanted to ride from Las Vegas to Zion National Park. The last thing we wanted to do was join the masses of steel and rubber on the freeway, but there was no getting around it. We entered the on-ramp to make the best of it.

Making the best of freeway riding wasn't easy. All the junk created by vehicles whizzing past at seventy-five mph creates havoc for bike tires. Both my bike and the triple ended up with flats from the little wires spit out by thousands of steel-belted tires. To add insult to injury, I somehow managed to leave my helmet behind when we stopped for groceries, so had to turn around and pedal a couple miles back to retrieve it.

We were pedaling hard to reach a place where we could camp. Exits were few and far between and, while on the interstate, we were held hostage by wire fences on either side.

"Nancy!" John shouted at me to be heard over the din of the highway. "That rainstorm is coming fast! We can't make it to the next exit."

"We have to!" I shouted back. "We can't camp here. We're right on the interstate!"

"We don't have a choice," he replied. "It's almost dark and that rainstorm will be here in a few minutes!" We looked eastward where we could see lightning flashing with scary regularity.

"There's no way we can camp here," I shouted back. "We'll just have to go until we get to the next exit. Those fences along the highway to keep the animals out are trapping us in. There's no place to pitch the tent."

In the end, John managed to find a decent spot to pitch our tent about twenty feet off the freeway behind a little hillock. Given our circumstances as hostages of the interstate, we considered ourselves lucky that we were, at least, hidden from the highway and had a flat spot for the tent. And that we managed to get camp set up before Mother Nature unleashed her fury.

A few minutes after climbing in for the evening, we heard the first pitter-patters of rain on the tent. We listened as nature's orchestra ramped up the intensity to include deafening thunder claps and watched the tent light up as bright bolts of lightning flashed in the sky. Rain pummeled our nylon shelter and wind distorted our tent like the contortionist we saw as we waited in line for a magic show in Vegas. We fell asleep hoping and praying our tent was up to the challenge it was faced with.

"We're stuck, Nancy," John proclaimed the following morning when he climbed out of the tent. "This doesn't look good. The sky is still filled with dark gray rain clouds, and it'll be raining here in a few minutes. We can't go on – if we do everything will be soaked."

"We don't have a choice," I responded as I emerged from the tent. "We don't have much food, and very little water. I mean – we're right next to the interstate for God's sake! We can't hang out here all day!"

"Well, I'll tell you one thing. I'm not packing up right now. That rain storm over there will be here within thirty minutes and there is no way we can get everything packed before that. Besides, even if we were to try to pack up now, all we would manage to do is get all our dry stuff wet. The tent fly is soaked, but the tent itself is okay. If we pack it all together, we'll end up with the whole thing being drenched. It's stupid to pack up like this!"

We climbed back in the tent to wait for the coming rain storm to pass.

We ended up spending the entire day and that night right there behind our little hillock twenty feet from the interstate. Shower after shower passed, so we holed up in our tent reading, playing cards, and doing beadwork while listening to the hum of rubber

In order to avoid riding in the rain we camped just yards from the interstate. We were stuck there for a whole day and could only leave the tent for short stretches between showers.

on pavement all day. We joked about how lucky we were to be serenaded by the melody of passing cars while waiting for the rain to pass.

Between thunder showers, the four of us emerged from our cocoon and hung around outside for a few minutes, eating the last few morsels of food I had stashed in my panniers and watching our water dwindle away. I regretted not having a means of capturing the rain water to refill our bottles.

By the following morning the rain had passed and we happily packed all our belongings onto our iron maidens and took off to brave the jungle of interstate traffic once again. As miserable as riding on the freeway was, we all agreed that it brought us to a magical place – Zion National Park.

Temperatures plummeted while we were in Zion, yet the spectacular views made it all worthwhile. We curled up in our down cocoons at night, and piled on every layer of clothing we could find to brave the chilly mornings. During the day, however, the fall temps were perfect for hiking and exploring the park. We spent a few days wandering the many trails cris-scrossing the park and thoroughly enjoyed the break from cycling.

Dear Grandma,

When we woke up this morning it was ice cold. We put on lots of layers of clothes. We had to go through a tunnel but bikes weren't allowed in so we hitched a ride in a pick-up. We saw lots of swirls and twirls in the rocks. It was cool. We also saw a checker-board mesa. It was really neat too. We saw buffalo and two snakes. We are going to have a fire tonight. It is going to be very cold.

Love, Davy

Oh my! I thought as I cycled out of Zion. *I'm speechless. Yes, me – the one dubbed Chatty McChatter McChattington by my boys – I'm speechless.* I tried all day to come up with words to describe the whirly, twirly, swirly sandstone formations we rode through that day, but consistently came up empty-handed. I wanted to write home to Mom and describe our surroundings, but somehow couldn't find the right words.

I thought of "breathtakingly beautiful" but that was too trite; "stunningly gorgeous" was too blah; "exquisitely carved by the Creator" was too gushy; "uncommonly delicious" – that might have worked, but it wasn't cookies I was talking about; "absotively, posilutely, spectacularly stupendous" was too tongue-twisty. So there it was. I was officially speechless for perhaps the first time in my life.

We had prepared for a cold ride, but the gods were with us and warmed things up considerably. Just a few weeks earlier we had cycled in the early mornings and late afternoons to avoid the sweltering heat of Death Valley. Now the only comfortable time to ride was the middle of the day. We realized we needed to come up with some kind of plan to deal with the cold, but we weren't at all sure what that plan would be.

In some ways it was frustrating – we had finally settled into a nice comfortable rhythm and knew what we were doing. And then the rules all changed and we were back to square one. And yet that was what made the trip

A warm fire was wonderful on bone-chilling mornings.

so fun and exciting – the fact that every day was different and we never knew what kind of challenges our days would bring.

Cold continued to be the word of the day as we slowly made our way across the Colorado Plateau in Southern Utah. We sought out places to pitch our tent based on availability of wood for campfires. All evening we huddled around the fire before making a mad dash to our sleeping bags. John braved early morning frosts to get a fire lit for me and the boys, so all we had to do was make another mad dash back to the fire upon waking.

Breaking camp and packing the bikes was excruciatingly slow as John and I could only work a few minutes before needing to thaw out our frozen fingers over the flames. Once we were ready to go, we wrapped the boys in every scrap of clothing we could find and dragged them away from the fire and onto the bike.

Our cycling hours were limited to just a few in the middle of the day. We took advantage of that time and pedaled hard, trying to get to the Grand Canyon and then off the plateau before the full blast of winter hit us. The cold was sapping our energy and making life difficult, but we slowly made progress through the Navajo Reservation.

One day things were just blah. The sky was dark and dreary and overcast. We were climbing a twenty-mile hill. We were cold and uncomfortable. As we took breaks by the side of the road, the four of us sat quietly rather than chatting as usual. Blah.

By late afternoon a rainstorm was imminent. We were near the top of a pass at 6500 feet, it was cold, and we wanted to get to a lower elevation to camp. Then it started to sprinkle.

"John!" I called to him ahead of me. "It's raining! Let's stop to bag everything."

"It's not raining hard yet," he shouted back. "Let's just go! We're close to the top of the pass – hopefully we can make it down before the storm really hits. If we stop now we'll never make it! Let's just ride as fast as we can."

We crested the pass and headed down – with rain drops accumulating on our jackets. We didn't have rain pants, only jackets. John and I could deal with cold, but if the kids got wet and cold, they would be miserable. They were both wearing thick cotton sweatpants which would never dry and we knew we couldn't get them wet. We raced down the pass and the whole time I was thinking, *Gotta protect the kids... can't let them get wet... we need shelter...* We were in the middle of the Navajo Reservation and there was no shelter. Fortunately, by the time we dropped down to a normal elevation the rain had stopped, although we knew a major rainstorm wasn't far away.

We rode a few more miles through Navajo land looking for a place to camp. There were houses scattered here and there everywhere, but John finally managed to find a deserted house separated from the rest. We darted behind the abandoned house and quickly set up camp – right next to a dry river bed. We knew that, with the threat of rain it might not be a dry river bed in the morning. We climbed into our tent knowing that if we heard the roar of a flash flood we needed to scramble.

At some point in the wee hours of the morning I sat up and yelled, "John! Get me a flashlight!"

"Huh?" he mumbled.

"I'm gonna throw up!" I shouted as I frantically unzipped the tent. "Get me a flashlight!"

I slipped on my shoes, unzipped the fly, grabbed the flashlight and headed out. I made it a grand total of eight feet before emptying my gut.

"Aw, Nancy," John complained, "you could have gone farther away." I should have barfed on him.

I crawled back in my sleeping bag shivering uncontrollably. An hour later I had managed to stop shaking, just in time for diarrhea to hit. I scrambled back outside into the cold and rain.

By morning I was exhausted. I had been up the entire night making mad dashes out of the tent into the bitter cold and felt like crap. Fortunately, the rain had passed. As much as I wanted to curl up and go to sleep, I knew as well as John did that we couldn't stay. We were camped behind an abandoned house on Navajo land and we had no food or water. We needed to continue on.

There isn't much worse than being sick and needing to ride. But having to ride uphill and against the wind while sick certainly was worse and I fought for each pedal stroke. After what I thought was ten or twelve miles, I glanced at the odometer. It said four miles. I could have sworn it was lying.

About sixty miles later (eleven miles according to the lying odometer) I started feeling a bit better and the wind shifted into a crosswind. We made fairly good time into a small village where we bought lunch. As the four of us stood outside the small store munching on burritos and potato chips, John looked back and noticed a nasty storm off in the distance.

"Good thing the wind is a cross-wind," he commented. "If it was a tail wind that storm would be heading right for us."

Less than a minute later the wind shifted into a direct tail wind and the temperature dropped considerably. We jumped on our bikes and rode like the wind! We had never gone so fast – ever! Before long sand was blowing along the road in huge gusts. Shortly thereafter it wasn't even gusts – just a solid steady stream of dust. Visibility was next to nothing as we cruised effortlessly at thirty miles per hour praying to God above there were no pot holes in the road.

We tried to stop and wait out the storm, but the howling wind was too strong. We couldn't even stand still without being blown over. We climbed back on our bikes and allowed the wind to push us onwards.

After the fastest thirty miles on record, we pulled into the trading post in Cameron. When John smiled I could see his grit-covered teeth, and I was sure mine were just as bad. Everything else was coated with a thick layer of dust. But we had survived the sandstorm, and had gotten ourselves to a safe place. We had a lot to be thankful for.

We wandered around the trading post shellshocked but safe.

Dear Grandma,

We went through a very bad sandstorm. We went over thirty-five miles per hour and got dust all over us. We were very scared. We stopped at a store and didn't leave until the storm was over. We camped behind a Chevron and superstore. We took showers. Daryl got lost again when he tried to find the bathroom, but we found him after not too much time.

Love, Davy

The next day we were climbing to the Grand Canyon at last. It had been nearly a thousand miles since we left the coast, and our destination was finally within reach. The four of us were giddy with excitement, knowing we would soon be at one of the most spectacular places on Earth.

"Hey, Mom!" Davy called to me as we ground our way up the hill. "I'm hungry."

I pulled out some carrots for him to munch on as we climbed.

A short while later we took a break on the side of the road and Davy crawled into my lap. "I'm hungry, Mom," he said. "Very hungry."

I handed him some more carrots.

A few miles from the entrance to the National Park, we pulled into the forest to camp for the night.

"I'm really, really hungry," Davy complained as we set up the tent. I pulled out the carrots again.

A while later, after we had camp set up and organized for the night, I made peanut butter and jelly tortillas. Davy took one bite and set it down. "I'm really hungry, but I just can't eat." He curled up in my lap again.

A few seconds later, he jumped off my lap and barfed up a whole lot of carrot soup. I realized Davy had never thrown up before – ever. The poor kid had been feeling badly for hours, but had no idea what was going on. All he knew was that his stomach hurt, and that had always meant hunger in the past. Now he knew.

All evening we sat around the fire with Davy curled up on my lap. Every once in a while he would leap up and make a mad dash to the bushes for another round of throwing up. John and I grew more and more concerned – the last thing we wanted was a bunch of carrot puke in the tent.

"Listen, sweetie," I told Davy before we went to bed. "If you need to throw up in the night, I need you to shout out really loudly, 'I need to throw up!' okay?"

"Yeah," he replied. "I can do that."

"John," I continued. "If he needs to throw up, you open the tent door while I'm turning on the flashlight. Davy – all you need to do is scramble outside as fast as you can. Don't even take the time to put on your shoes – just go! I'll follow right after you with your shoes, okay?"

Davy rose to the challenge. When the moment came, he knew exactly what to do and did it admirably. He scrambled out of the tent into sub-freezing temperatures time and time again.

The amazing thing was that Daryl, too, knew exactly what to do. So when *he* needed to barf a few hours later, he sounded the alarm and we all reacted just as planned – while Davy slept peacefully.

The following morning I crawled out of our frost-covered tent into the bitter cold Arizona desert and surveyed my surroundings. As my eyes landed on the many frozen piles of puke dotting the ground, I wondered, for perhaps the millionth time in the past four months, just why I was there. What could possibly have possessed me to haul my sons around North America on bicycles? What kind of madness caused me to subject my darling boys to numerous mad dashes out of the tent in sub-freezing temperatures to barf in the woods? What kind of mother was I anyway?

My questions were answered a few hours later when we arrived at the Grand Canyon and marveled at Mother Nature's

Daryl enjoyed making smoke figures as he played with Ninja sticks.

amazingly exquisite handiwork. Yes, it was all worth it. All our frozen fingers and tired legs, puke runs in the middle of the night and being sandblasted in the desert – they were all just a small part of our adventure. The magic of our family being together and exploring our world was more than worth it all. Each and every one of us knew there was no going back.

Dear Grandma,

We took a class about the formation of the Grand Canyon. We learned it took almost two billion years to form. All you have to do to remember the process is to remember **DUDE**.

The **D in DUDE** stands for the **deposition** of rock. Once there was a swamp and there was a lot of mud at the bottom of the swamp. Eventually the mud turned into shale. Then there was a desert. After a long time the sand turned to a lot of sandstone. Where there was a shallow ocean covering the Grand Canyon we got limestone. But do you know what they all have in common? They were all formed at sea level.

The **U in DUDE** stands for the **uplifting** of rock. The uplifting of rock had to do with plate tectonics. The oceanic plate was thin but heavy, and the continental plate was thick but light. The oceanic plate went under the continental plate, pushing it up, forming the Colorado Plateau. But do you know what is weird about the Colorado Plateau? It is flat!

The **second D in DUDE** stands for **downcutting** of rock. It took the Colorado River six million years to cut the rock. The Colorado River goes very fast. It drags rocks and sediment out to the ocean. It makes the depth of the canyon.

*E in DUDE stands for **erosion** of rock. Rain, floods, and slides happen, which push other rock which makes the canyon wider.*

DUDE is still happening today. In the next five million years the canyon will keep getting wider and wider until you will not be able to see the other side.

Stay tuned: Big Cliff National Park coming in five million years!

Love, Davy & Daryl

It was Halloween. We were camped fifty miles north of Williams, Arizona and wanted to get to town so the boys could go trick or treating. The way we figured it, fifty miles wouldn't be too bad. But we didn't count on the head wind – a *stiff* head-wind. We battled and battled until John didn't think he could battle any more.

The kids and I urged him on, determined to get to town before evening. The kids pedaled like never before, but the bulk of the burden still rested on John's shoulders. I could see the fatigue in his eyes, his shoulders, and his demeanor. He occasionally slumped off the bike and collapsed to the ground for a break, but always managed to climb back on to continue his heroic efforts.

Three miles from town I suggested camping in the forest and the kids and I walk into town. John all too readily agreed and we headed off the road into the trees. The boys and I grabbed what we needed and headed out, while John set the tent up to relax for the evening.

The three of us hitched a ride to civilization and began our forays into Halloween in a strange town. We stumbled into a celebration at a church and an hour later walked out with a plateful of cupcakes and *two* whole pies, in addition to a bunch of candies and toys.

The boys took off running from house to house and it wasn't long before their bags were full of candy. We emptied them into the backpack I was carrying. They filled the bags again in no time.

It was late when the boys decided they had enough booty. My backpack was stuffed to the point where we had to hand-feed candies piece by piece through a tiny opening in the zipper. Each kid carried a plastic grocery bag stuffed to the very tippy top. And I carried two pies and a plate of cupcakes. We wearily made our way back to the main road to hitch a ride to the middle of nowhere.

"You want to get out *here*?" the driver asked when we reached the spot where John was camped in the woods. "There's absolutely nothing around for miles!"

"Except our tent somewhere back in those trees," I replied.

The boys and I followed a dirt road for a ways until we spied a particular sign we had noted as a landmark, then turned right and began counting our steps. On our way out we had counted steps to determine just how far we needed to go knowing that, in the pitch blackness of a moonless night, we wouldn't be able to see the tent at all. We stumbled over logs and ran into trees, but eventually we found John and the tent.

"Daddy! Daddy!" the kids yelled as we made our way back into the depths of the forest. "Daddy! You wouldn't believe what we got!"

John took a quick look at the enormous haul. "What did you guys do? How in the heck do you expect to carry all this crap on the bikes? Our panniers are stuffed already!"

We decided we would deal with it in the morning and mummified ourselves in our sleeping bags.

The following morning was cold. Very cold. Our water bottles were frozen solid, as were our cupcakes and pies. We hacked out pieces of pie the best we could and ate them for breakfast. We froze our teeth on frozen icing. There was no liquid water to brush our teeth with so we simply loaded everything up and headed to town. The kids were in heaven, and John and I simply shook our shook our heads in wonder. Somehow I don't think either of us ever considered a Halloween like that before we pedaled away from home!

We were getting tired of cold. We had finally figured out how to deal with it, but that didn't mean we enjoyed it. I was getting tired of having to be zipped into my sleeping bag each night and was looking forward to the night when I would be able to use the bag as a blanket again. I had owned that sleeping bag for many years and had never been zipped into it until the last couple of weeks. I generally used my bag as a blanket – a mighty fine blanket at that. I typically flung it over me and I could toss and turn to my heart's content. I could curl up, or stretch out, or tuck one leg up and leave the other extended, arms in or out.

Having the bag zipped up, on the other hand, wasn't quite the same. It was kind of like cramming pickled pig's feet in a jar, sardines in a can, or Ethiopians in a bus. It just wasn't comfy. My legs had to work in tandem, turning over required super-human efforts, and the little hole for my face never seemed to stay at my face and it wasn't easy breathing through my ears. I couldn't wait to drop down off the plateau to warmer temperatures.

In time we descended off the Colorado plateau and entered Saguaro country. The magnificent cactus signified warmth for us, and we rejoiced every time we passed by them. We quickly shed our many layers of clothing until, once again, we wore only shorts and t-shirts. We very happily changed our routine this time.

Dear Grandma,

We are now in Joshua Tree National Park. We were talking about rock climbing our whole way to the campsite. When we arrived, we immediately set off for The Rocky Tour. There was a great big humongous granite rock near the campground, and we wanted to climb to the top of it. We didn't expect the climb to be so hard. Mommy got stabbed by a barrel cactus as we hiked and her leg was bleeding.

Two times we set off to see if we could get up onto the rock. Failure. Finally we found our way up. It was on a steep face. We got up by using the cracks in it. We went through a tunnel and slowly up to the top of the ridge to wait for Daddy. The tunnel was such a small hole that it was hard for Daddy to get through. We got to the top of the ridge and over a rock we called "The Mitten." Then we thought we saw a way to make it to the tippy-top but we couldn't.

Daddy came, and we talked about how to get up. We saw some people on top, so we said, "Somebody got up. We can go the way they did!"

Daddy said, "Yeah. They got up from there." He pointed in the direction we just came from.

So we went there. We walked on a foot-wide cliff. From there you have to jump over an empty spot and climb up. But Daddy wouldn't let us. We watched some other people climb up. We went to that place but it was too dangerous to get to the very tippy-top. So we sat there for a while then tried to get back down. We went to The Mitten.

Daddy said it wasn't the right way. We insisted it was the right way. Daddy sent me down a steep path to see if it was the tunnel. It wasn't. So Daddy went over The Mitten. There was a crack, but he couldn't use it to get up. We finally had to pull him up. When we got him up we set off for the face. The face wasn't half as hard as I expected.

When we got down, Daddy took us for a shortcut.

Love, Davy

"Nancy!" John whispered in the middle of the night as we slept under the stars. "There's something in your bike. I hear it scrambling around over there."

I dragged myself out of my sleeping bag and stumbled over, expecting some little chipmunk-y creature. Nothing was there, but what I found shocked the daylights out of me!

This wasn't some itty-bitty critter – this was a great big creature with claws big enough to slash gigantic holes in the plastic bag that, at one time, had held our breakfast. All that remained was part of the salami wrapper – the salami and cheese were conspicuously absent. Our cream cheese, however, seemed to have escaped the creature's jowls. I double-bagged the cream cheese (which, unfortunately, was covered with salami juice), and strapped it on top of my bike rack. Then I closed up all my panniers as securely as possible and moved my bike next to John (who happens to be a very light sleeper). I climbed back in bed and drifted off to dreamland once again.

A few minutes later John called out again – the creature was back. John pulled out his flashlight and shined it to where my bike had been just a few minutes before. A great big gray fox stared right back from less than twenty feet away. The fox stared at us for a few moments as though deciding what kind of threat level we presented. Evidently, he concluded we were no threat at all and promptly returned to prowling. John and I looked at each other in amazement. We were stunned. All along, we had thought wild creatures were supposed to be scared of humans!

"What's going on?" Davy asked, as he sat up to join John and me as we watched the fox circle our campsite.

"Look over there, sweetie," I replied. "That fox is beautiful. But I'm also scared – wild animals shouldn't be this close to humans. I don't know if this guy has rabies or what. I never dreamed he would get this close to us."

John gathered a pile of rocks and a couple of big sticks for us to use in defense should the fox attack. He placed a big sticker bush right on top of the cream cheese on my bike and carefully positioned the backpack (with additional food in it) at Daryl's feet. We both figured that, if the fox was brave enough to raid the food this close to us, John would wake up. The whole time John was up and wandering around, the fox was never far. At one point the creature came to within seven feet of Davy and me.

Deciding our food stash was secure, we finally slept.

A few hours later, the sun came up and John climbed out of bed. "Nancy!" he exclaimed. "The fox got it after all!" Our cream cheese had vanished. Our backpack had been dragged a good twenty feet from us, although the fox hadn't been able to open it. We never did figure out how that fox managed to get the cream cheese, while leaving the sticker bush untouched, but we vowed to pack our food more securely in the future.

> Dear Grandma,
>
> We visited Borrego Springs State Park and learned a lot! A rattle of a rattlesnake does not tell the age of the rattlesnake. The reason is because the rattles break easy and rattlesnakes only shed once a year. They can only grow a rattle when they shed. Rattlesnakes can unhinge their jaws so they can eat their prey whole. The reason rattlesnakes stick their tongues out is to smell. Rattlesnakes can feel vibrations on the ground and can sense heat in the air. A lot of desert snakes are not poisonous.
>
> Love, Daryl

"What would you say about Disneyland tomorrow?" I asked my boys as we lounged in the hot tub behind the house of our hosts in San Diego.

"Disneyland? Really? Can we go?"

"You bet! Remember I promised way back in Oregon? Now we're here – we can head up there tomorrow."

The boys didn't remember my promise at all. At the time, in the middle of the desert in Oregon, the thought of visiting Disneyland was a huge motivator. Now, they had seen the magic of bike touring and didn't need an external motivator like Mickey. Still, I had promised and intended to carry through on my promise.

Our hosts, Dave and Anne, graciously lent us their car for the day so we could get to the Magic Kingdom quickly. The boys had a blast on Space Mountain and the other rides. They trained as Jedi and danced with Mickey Mouse.

After so long in Mother Nature's handiwork, it was a little slice of heaven to leave nature behind and play with cartoon characters for a day. It was a bit of American decadence before heading south of the border for a whole new experience.

Thorny Fantasyland

Thanksgiving was over and we were ready for a new challenge. We slowly made our way through the mess and mayhem of the border region, obtained Mexican visas, and crossed the border. We could only hope our five months on the road had adequately prepared us for what we would face in a new country. The four of us passed into the new world with trepidation and excitement, not knowing exactly how we should be feeling.

As we pedaled away from the border station, we found ourselves funneled onto a busy expressway with no shoulder. Cars and trucks buzzed past, making communication between us impossible. John and I, being new to Tijuana, had no idea which way we should be going and blindly pedaled on, hoping to find a way to exit the expressway. Drivers were, for the most part, courteous and gave us a wide berth, but when another lane merged from the right we were in trouble. We needed to pass through that lane of traffic to get to the nearly non-existent shoulder on the far right side of the road, but getting through the unbroken line of vehicles was a near impossibility.

John, concentrating fully simply on controlling the triple, couldn't even look behind as he cycled ahead of me sandwiched between two lanes of traffic traveling at nearly seventy miles per hour. I frantically signaled drivers to stop and let us cross the lane, but car after car zoomed past. At last a police car slowed down behind us to hold up traffic so we crossed the lane and continue pedaling.

We waited for the police car to pass so we could wave a quick "Thank you!" but they never passed. When I finally felt stable enough to take a peek behind, I discovered the police car right behind us with its lights flashing.

"John!" I shouted over the din of highway traffic. "A police car is giving us an escort!"

Knowing the police were behind us, we relaxed and pedaled through the busy, narrow section of highway. Eventually the road widened to include a wide shoulder and started climbing a steep hill. The police turned on their loud speaker, pulled up next to us and broadcast, "Goodbye! Good luck!"

John and I both shouted, "*Gracias!*" and we were on our own.

A few miles later, we approached the toll booth to officially enter the expressway. A man ran toward us waving his arms. "*No bicicleta!*" he proclaimed. "*Se prohibe bicicleta! Bicicleta - no!*"

I understood precisely that the man was trying to tell me bikes were not allowed on the tollway, but decided to play the ignorant American tourist and simply replied, "Ensenada this way, no?"

"*Bicicleta no!*"

"This way to Ensenada?"

In the end our ignorant American ploy failed. He went to find an English speaker. We decided it was time to lie.

"We tried the old highway yesterday," we fibbed, "but it was too narrow and busy, and there is no shoulder." The entire group of highway officials who had congregated around us nodded. "So we talked with the police and they suggested we come this way." In reality, it had been other cyclists who had recommended the toll road.

After conferring for what seemed like ages, they finally agreed the toll road was safer, agreed to let us pass, and said they would call the toll booth ahead to notify the workers there.

83

A few minutes later we approached the toll booth and a worker flagged us down. "The gentlemen back there called to notify us to allow you to pass. We want to do that, but we have a problem."

My mind started racing. *How can we get around this one?*

"We have cameras here. If we let you go through, it will be caught on camera and we will get in trouble. So we will have to do some maneuvering."

What kind of "maneuvering" is he talking about?

"You see that red retaining wall over on the other side of the expressway?" he asked. "We have to go behind that." All I saw was a solid wall of dirt. "No worry. I will direct you," he assured us.

We crossed six lanes of traffic, approached the embankment, and stood there looking at where we needed to go – eight feet up, with a four-foot vertical cliff. My bike would be difficult to get up. John's bike? Almost impossible. One thing we had learned on our journey was that we could do most things; the impossible simply took longer. This was no exception.

John and I set about the task of taking off the trailer and unstrapping our gear. The kids set off with our lighter bags and panniers, while John, the highway man and I managed to get the bikes up the embankment. We walked along a narrow pathway behind the retaining wall, crossed a six-inch-wide bridge over a ditch, and climbed back down to the highway. After crossing all six lanes of traffic once again, we reassembled the bikes and were about to take off. The whole process of getting past the toll booth had taken nearly two hours.

Then the officials appeared. In a van. Riffraff don't drive vans. *This is it. The gig is up. We'll be fined $500 and sent back.*

John pulled out all the stops and began to schmooze for all he was worth. With a huge smile plastered on his face he greeted the officials. "Yes. Yes, we are going to Ensenada. Actually we'll go to La Paz, then to Mazatlan. Yes, with the children. From Idaho. Five months..." All the while grinning like the Cheshire cat and oozing charm and schmooze.

Schmoozing the highway officials paid off. They let us go! Cyclists weren't allowed on the toll road through Mexico, but we wanted to cycle it as it had a shoulder.

Finally the magic words came: "Enjoy your trip. Be careful!" and they climbed back in their van.

We were free to go, but we faced on one more problem. We stood on the side of the tollway with a man who just helped us break the law and we were totally ignorant about protocol. Had he helped us just to be nice? Should we pay him off? How much would one pay an official who willingly broke the law for you? John finally turned and asked, "Can we pay you?"

"For what?" he replied.

"For helping us. We want to help you."

"No. No, I am happy to help. You help me when I go to your country."

"Yes, of course. We will help you when you come to Idaho. Thank you. Thank you very much."

We continued on our way.

Twenty five kilometers later we approached another toll booth. A man motioned us up onto a sidewalk to avoid the cameras. We lifted the bikes up, walked fifty meters, and lifted the bikes back down.

As we mounted our cycles and prepared to leave we waved goodbye to a mob of eight or nine policemen, while blatantly disregarding the "No Bicycles" sign above our heads.

We realized we had a lot to learn about how things were done in Mexico.

Dear Grandma,

We made it to Mexico. I cannot read the signs or understand people. Only Mommy can do those because she speaks Spanish. They have a lot of corn tortillas here, but I like flour tortillas better. I need a lot of cheese on my corn tortilla or it will not taste good. The money in Mexico is pesos. I'm not used to using pesos yet.

Love, Daryl

By the next day we were pros. As we approached toll booths, men came running frantically trying to intercept us before it was too late. By then we knew the drill and lifted our bikes up on the sidewalk to walk to the other side of the toll booths, where we picked the bikes up again to get them off the sidewalk. Nobody cared that we rode on the tollway; they just didn't want us to get picked up by the cameras.

Within a few days we came to the end of the tollway and continued south on a two-lane country road passing through a narrow river valley with mountains on either side. Although the road was narrow with no shoulder, it wasn't a problem at all. Drivers were respectful and gave us wide berth and we thoroughly enjoyed a relaxing ride.

As nightfall approached, we began searching for spot for our tent. One of the drawbacks of a narrow valley is that there aren't a whole lot of flat places at all, let alone one large enough to accommodate a four-person tent. It was getting late and there wasn't much daylight left and we were starting to worry – we weren't sure how long the narrow valley was, but it looked even narrower and steeper up ahead. Then we saw a tree farm with a lot of flat space. It was perfect. It was also private property.

On the other side of the fence, we could see men chopping down trees. I walked over to them. "Do you guys think we could possibly put our tent in here tonight?" I asked in Spanish.

"You'll have to talk with the owner," they replied. "He should be here in thirty minutes."

We were in a quandary. As we looked ahead, we could see the road for a mile or so. There was certainly no place to camp in that stretch of road. If we waited in hopes of a perfect spot in the tree farm, it would be too late to find anything else should the owner not allow us to stay. On the other hand, if we left and looked for something else, we may or may not find something, and we would have abandoned all hopes of the perfect tree farm. In the end, we waited.

Fortunately, the owner had no problem with us staying so we settled in for the night in a perfect little grassy spot amongst the trees.

All too soon morning arrived and we discovered that our perfect campsite ended up being not quite so perfect after all. It was a nice spot in a small grove of trees on a narrow strip of grass between a eucalyptus tree farm and an open field which had recently been plowed and prepared for planting (which translated to a great big field of loose dirt).

As I prepared dinner the night before in our ideal spot in our small grove of trees I had noticed the wind kicking up quite a dust cloud. I thought, *I'm sure glad I'm here, sheltered by these wonderful trees, rather than out there in all that dust.*

A couple of hours later, once we were all snuggled in warm and cozy, the wind picked up in earnest. It whistled and howled through the trees all night long, and it picked up buckets of dust from the freshly-plowed field.

It seemed like the wind funneled every single bucketful of dirt right down onto our little campsite. In the morning we awoke to find a thick layer of dirt covering everything like fine gray snow. Dirt had penetrated through the mesh windows of the tent, covering our sleeping bags with a gritty film. Our tent was blanketed with a fine gray tapestry. Our bikes, panniers, helmets, sunglasses, *everything* was covered with dust. What a mess! What a great big, colossal mess! The mess to end all messes. The mother of them all.

Fortunately we had closed all our panniers but one. That one was filled with dirt. John and I spent an hour or so cleaning up the best we could and set off, feeling that the day could only get better. After all, things couldn't possibly get any worse – or could they?

The couple of miles of climbing we had seen the previous evening turned out to be the start of a full-blown pass up a steep incline on a narrow, windy road with no shoulder. Fortunately, the drivers were courteous, but a few blind corners caused a bit of concern. But by far the most concern was caused by wind.

There isn't much worse than a headwind. It's like climbing a hill with no summit. It's like fighting an unbeatable foe. No matter how many hours you battle or how valiantly you fight, you know you will never claim victory. We battled that foe all morning – climbing the pass, down the pass, around the corners. He never let us rest.

By noon we had made it a grand total of twenty miles and stopped in San Vicente for lunch. Our intention was to eat and continue on, but the demoralizing effect of the headwind had beaten us down. We checked into a hotel and called it a day.

We were pedaling south in Baja through an especially remote and mountainous region and, as my legs pumped, I pondered our relatively short supply of water. It was approximately seventy miles to the nearest town; seventy miles of difficult terrain and high heat. Seventy miles of needing an awful lot of water and, I feared, our meager water supplies were no match for the job.

As we laboriously pumped up yet another mountain pass, two men flagged us over and plied us with bottles of Gatorade, which we very happily accepted. We stood there, dripping sweat and

chugging Gatorade, while Balo and Ole introduced themselves.

"We first saw you back in Ensenada," Ole told us. "We could tell from your bikes that you were going a long way. So this morning, before we left town, we bought a case of Gatorade for you."

Our mouths gaped open in astonishment.

"I know the Gatorade is too heavy to carry, so this is what we're going to do: every fifteen or twenty kilometers we'll build a rock cairn like this." Ole built up a pile of rocks on the side of the road. "Then we'll go a few meters back from the road and hide four bottles of Gatorade under a bush or behind a rock."

By that point our jaws were hanging down around our belly buttons.

"Okay?" he asked. "Every fifteen or twenty kilometers you'll find a rock cairn. Near there will be four Gatorades."

We nodded our heads, unable to speak.

Balo walked over to a cooler and brought out a Ziploc baggie with a big foil-wrapped something and a bunch of napkins inside. "The Gatorade we can hide on the road for you. But these tamales we can't. You'll have to eat these soon."

I picked my jaw up off the ground and gratefully accepted the bag of tamales.

A mile or so later we found a small patch of shade, sat down to eat our tamales, and I knew I had arrived. Nirvana... utopia... heaven... whatever you want to call it... I was there. That had to rate right up there as the all-time best lunch consumed on the side of the road!

Licking our lips and fingers to get every last tasty morsel, we climbed back on our bikes to begin the treasure hunt. We kept our eyes peeled for a rock cairn, and our boys were giddy with excitement as they scanned the roadside for signs of cairns. When we finally found a pile, the boys jumped off the bike and began searching.

"Mommy!" they squealed in delight when the spied four brightly colored bottles hidden under a bush like baby birds waiting for their mother. "We found it!"

Their delight never dimmed, and each time we discovered another stash the four of us gratefully climbed off our bikes and enjoyed the refreshing liquid in the shade of an enormous cardon cactus.

Dear Grandma,

We had a very hilly day today. We were either going up or down, but never flat, all day. It really wore me out. There were some people that stopped and gave us a whole bunch of Gatorade and granola bars. But there was only one problem. We could not carry all of the Gatorade. They said they would make rock piles by the road. We would go straight back and find some hidden Gatorade. We found one pack so far. They also gave us some tamales. They were good. We camped in a ranch. On the ranch if you wander back enough you get killed by guard dogs.

Love, Daryl

"That way," he said as he languorously pointed south. All I could see was the grin, blazing through the sun's noontime rays. I knew the Cheshire Cat was lurking there, perched upon a graceful arm of a giant cardon cactus. I pondered the strangeness of a grin without a cat and looked about in wonder. Was I seeing things? Or had I honestly pedaled my way into the most intriguing landscape on Earth?

We had stumbled into *Valle de los Cirios*, and I felt exactly how I imagine Alice felt as she took those first tentative steps into Wonderland. I marveled at impossibly absurd boojum trees extending fifty feet into the air and at the sheer variety and density of cacti scattered about. The ground was covered so thoroughly and completely with various species of cacti that we struggled mightily to find a vacant spot large enough to accommodate our bicycles and tent in the evening.

But the real magic of the valley appeared the following day. We cycled around a corner and I fell headlong down a hole and ended up in Wonderland! I felt like Alice as I gazed in wonder at huge boulders strewn around as though they had been tossed by

Camping amongst the cacti in Baja was relaxing and a very unique experience.

a giant toddler. Nestled in the nooks and crannies between boulders we found cacti of every species imaginable. Enormous cardons, resembling their sister saguaros, towered majestically over the valley floor as though protecting its inhabitants with their enormous arms.

Alongside the cardons stood the almost silly-looking boojum trees, like gigantic upside-down fuzzy carrots with pathetic crowns perched haphazardly atop them. Hiding in the crevices of the rocks we found a multitude of other types of cactus. Along with the impossibly tall cardons and boojums, equally tiny cacti-like foxtail littered the ground, as well as cacti of every size and shape in between. Long skinny organ pipe cactus grew alongside short squatty barrel cactus.

Teddy bear cholla, with its detachable balls that tended to jump out and grab you, fought for space amongst the multitude of other plant life. Elephant trees, like miniature baobab trees transplanted from the African savanna, shaded rainbow cacti and a myriad of different species of yucca and century plants. It has been said over 125 different species of cactus can be found in the Baja, and I had little doubt that each and every one of them resided in *Valle de los Cirios*.

I was Alice exploring Wonderland as I pedaled my bike through the bizarre, magical landscape. Each new twist and turn of the road brought new wonders to behold and new sights to gaze upon. Granite boulders, as big as a house, served nicely as the Mad Hatter's table. I felt impossibly small and insignificant standing next to gigantic cardons, then the next moment I was impossibly huge towering over lesser cacti.

Old man cactus, with its dense shaggy spines like an old man's grizzly gray beard, reminded me of the King of Hearts. The queen's army was ready to attack, perched upon their steeds of galloping cactus with strong sharp spines as weapons. But the queen was conspicuous only in her absence.

I laughed out loud at the ridiculous boojum trees, and delighted in scrambling over and around massive boulders with my children in search of Wonderland's hidden spectacles. At one point a rabbit scurried away, and I could have sworn I heard him mumble, "I'm late! I'm late! For a very important date!"

Many miles later, as we pedaled away from *Valle de los Cirios* and the boojum trees and cardons grew progressively smaller (... or was I growing larger?), there was a part of me that wanted to turn around... to pedal back into the magical desert landscape in search of the elusive Queen of Hearts. But the rest of Baja beckoned. I heeded the call and realized Wonderland couldn't continue on forever. I reluctantly pedaled away.

"Ah, Mom... Do I hafta?" Davy grumbled. "I wanna play here some more."

I looked around, bewildered, at "here." "Here" was simply a plain ol' wide spot in the road. We had stopped there solely for the purpose of fixing a flat tire. For the boys, however, "here" had become a soccer field, and the many discarded plastic Coke bottles found littering the ground had turned into soccer balls. "Yes, honey," I sighed. "This flat tire set us back, and we need to get into town today. Please go get on the bike." The boys took off to score one last goal before reluctantly climbing on the bike behind their father.

As we pedaled toward town I thought back upon the six months we had been on the road – on the hundreds of hours we had spent pedaling and the multitude of breaks we had taken on the sides of roads since we left home. And I thought about all my boys had learned in those months, learning that extended way beyond the traditional 3 R's of education.

At the beginning of the journey the kids dragged out miniature plastic aliens at each break. Their aliens fought battles and conquered new lands. By the next day rocks and sticks had become spaceships and distant planets which their aliens controlled. Within a few days, the aliens had been forgotten and their playthings were solely of the natural variety: rocks, sticks, leaves, and pinecones.

Our journey was magical in so many ways. For Davy and Daryl the magic lay in the dirt road that magically transformed into a soccer field, or the stones which became baseballs, or the old bottle perched on a fence post that converted into a target. The magic for them lay in the time to play and create, to dream and imagine, to explore and discover.

They became explorers discovering new and exciting territory in the dark caverns of tunnels beneath the road. They became major league baseball players pitching a no-hitter with rocks found on the side of the road. They became Power Rangers battling the evil forces with ninja sticks gathered from a fallen tree or engineers building complex dams of sand and stones.

Davy and Daryl perfected the fine art of taking full advantage of every second of break time. They became experts at immediately sizing up their environment and creating a game with whatever happened to be at hand. They may have spent their break throwing rocks at a cliff wall, trying to knock down a particular rock, or maybe they tried to capsize a raft (more than likely an old discarded plastic bottle) floating down a stream. Perhaps they found pinecones with which to fight World War 3 or old bottles that became bowling pins. My sons made forts with rocks and sand, they created playhouses in groves of trees, and they discovered ships hidden in the side of the road.

We pedaled into town, and I knew beyond a shadow of a doubt that our journey was the best gift we ever could have given our children.

One day as we cycled along the long lonely Baja highway, it suddenly wasn't quite so lonely. Although we had noticed there was a definite lack of cars on the road, we were surprised to see a solid row of cars lining the edge of the road.

We pedaled beside the cars watching passengers and drivers relax in the sun. Some lay in the seat with their feet hanging out the window; others played frisbee in a nearby field. A small group of drivers hung around chatting while seated on the hood of an ancient beat-up old car. Directly behind it sat an enormous RV.

Seeing the cars lined up waiting for gas to arrive made us very thankful for our mode of transportation.

"What's going on?" I asked John as we cycled side-by-side along the deserted road.

"I have no idea," he responded. "This is really bizarre."

A couple miles farther ahead we discovered the reason for all those cars parked by the side of the road: a gas shortage.

"We've been here in line for two days," one RV driver told us. "There is no gas anywhere in Baja right now, and we can't go on until we get some. They keep telling us the gas is coming, but I have no idea when it'll actually make it."

"I just need to get back to my village one hundred miles from here," added another driver. "The problem is that we just came in to town to buy food and left our cat locked in our house. The poor thing doesn't have any food or water and there is no way we can get back there. Fortunately, I just got hold of our neighbor and asked her to break in through a window to feed the cat."

As we milled around chatting with stranded travelers I couldn't help but think of their dependence on gasoline. They were getting around twenty miles per gallon, which translates to a lot of gas. And us? Our boys' fuel of choice was Oreo cookies – I figured we were getting maybe twenty miles per cookie, but at least we weren't stuck at a gas station waiting for the shipment to arrive.

"Deck the halls with boughs of holly..." We sang cheerfully with aging snowbirds as we sat around tables set up in an RV park. We had managed to find a Christmas potluck dinner to attend, so we showed up bearing a fancy pink plastic bowl filled with guacamole and a package of crackers. Everyone else brought wonderful homemade dishes, which they cooked in their ovens. We thoroughly enjoyed porking out on turkey and ham, potatoes, veggies, and pumpkin pies.

As we sat there stuffing our faces, John told stories to the party-goers. It was almost as though he was a young, famous explorer visiting a city after discovering wild and untamed lands. He was a rough and ragged adventurer, strong from months of traveling uncharted wilderness, regaling others with stories of his adventures. His audience of retired snowbirds who had escaped the frigid winters of the north listened attentively.

"A piñata!" Davy cried when he saw the bright, multi-colored ball hanging beside one of the RVs. "When do we get to break it?"

Our new-found friend, Joy, had purchased a piñata for the boys. They had a blast swinging a bat while blindfolded until they finally broke it open and made a mad dash for the candy strewn about the ground.

The boys were sure Santa wouldn't be able to find them out in the boonies of Baja, but Christmas had been a special holiday anyway. We made our way back to our little tent hidden in a grove of trees and fell asleep with visions of sugar plums dancing in our heads.

"Santa found us!" Davy shouted the following morning when he found presents piled at the foot of his sleeping bag. "Daryl! Santa came! He *is* real!"

"Mom, how much farther is it to La Paz?" Daryl asked as we took a break on the side of the road.

"It's pretty darn close now, sweetie," I replied. "We're so close we could walk from here if we needed to."

Daryl ran to his brother who was off in a field playing with old broken sticks. "Davy! Davy!" he shouted. "We're close enough to walk! We're almost to La Paz!"

The boys were in celebration mode. They jumped and shouted, they danced and whirled. They had made it. They had pedaled six thousand miles and had been seeing mileage signs for La Paz for well over seven hundred miles. And now, finally, La Paz was within reach. No longer was it some remote destination – it was here and now. After months of riding, we had reached our southern terminus.

After 6,000 miles we reached our southern terminus of La Paz. From here we took a ferry to mainland Mexico.

Approaching the top of yet another pass — big accomplishments!

We traveled the Oregon Trail and enjoyed relics from days gone by.

Temperatures cooled off significantly once we reached the Columbia River Gorge.

Lewis and Clark traveled along the Columbia River. The boys enjoyed playing on monuments along our path.

Hanging out waiting for rain to stop.

Relaxing in the San Juan Islands

Taking a nap while waiting for a ferry.

The enormous triple bike was dwarfed by gigantic redwood trees.

Hands-on learning at Fort Ross

Exploring Alcatraz prison

Exploring the Oregon coast

A foggy day along the coast

The boys loved playing on the beach. Every chance they had they headed down!

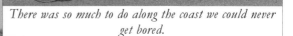

There was so much to do along the coast we could never get bored.

Playing ball in a campground. The boys had more energy than they knew what to do with.

We all enjoyed the peace and solitude of camping in the wild.

Red Rock just outside Las Vegas. It was an abrupt transition from remote countryside to massive city.

We had never seen Joshua trees before – lovely!

Playing King of the Rock

Flat tires were never fun, but on the side of the interstate, they were even less fun.

We love Zion National Park

Massive sandstorm moving in. Ten minutes later we were barreling down the road at thirty miles per hour with an incredible tailwind.

The Grand Canyon! It was beautiful, but so very cold.

Camping out at Joshua Tree National Park – very chilly night.

Into saguaro country!

We never tired of seeing Joshua trees

We got a special tour of the paleo lab at Anza Borrego State Park.

San Diego – the water was finally warm enough to enjoy!

A date farmer invited us to his farm.

We enjoyed all the sights at Disneyland.

A whole crew offered to help rebuild the bikes to get them ready for Mexico.

Davy

Daryl

Cycling Baja

Boojum trees were huge!

That's a long way to the tip of Baja!

Wonderland – this part of Baja was magical with many types of cactus.

Relaxing in a hostel. In the towns, we stayed in hostels but camped between them.

Baja was lovely, but all those cactus thorns were torture on our tires.

There was a wide variety of fruits and vegetables in the stalls.

Playing chess

John

Heading back out to the road after camping in the desert.

Our little rolling wagon train. Everything we needed we carried on our bikes.

Our friend, Harry. We met him in the Grand Canyon, then again at Carlsbad Caverns.

Davy was very proud of his fish!

Camping on the Appalachian Trail

Amish country

Horse carriages were more my speed.

The boys had a lot of fun exploring old bridges.

American History Days

Newfound friends

Covered bridges – a bit of Pennsylvanian history

Taking a break

Learning US history up close and personal at Gettysburg

Kids will be kids! Enjoying New York City

Cycling out of New York City was crazy!

Visiting the Statue of Liberty

Dangling Lightbulbs

"How is it, Nancy," John asked quietly as he glanced at my knee with a worried look. "How bad is it?"

I sat on the couch in our condo in Mazatlan with my leg elevated. The slightest movement caused searing pain to shoot through my knee and tears streamed down my face. The mental anguish was far worse than the physical pain.

John's mother, Anne, gently prodded my knee. Her many years of nursing experience provided no clues. My knee was a mystery. There was no obvious reason for the pain.

Anne had flown to Mazatlan for a week, and all five of us were enjoying our week in the lap of luxury. My mother had arranged for a condo on the beach for us, and we were relaxing in the luxurious accommodations. By day we hung out at the pool, went coconut bowling, played tennis, or took cooking lessons. By evening we sat around chatting or playing cards. It had been a wonderful time that we had all looked forward to for a long time.

All was going well until that moment when my knee went out. I was walking to the bedroom when I suddenly felt intense pain in my left knee. I froze, hugged the wall for support, and called out for John. He helped me hop to the couch where I sat, crying, trying to figure out what was happening.

The next week was a blur – a blur of painful steps, crutches, and doctor's visits. Eventually I managed to find a knee specialist who informed me I had calcification under my knee cap, which caused the kneecap to have trouble tracking. My kneecap had wandered off to the side, causing the pain.

"Don't worry," the doctor told me. "It'll get better. The kneecap is back in alignment now, so just give it time for the inflammation to go down. You might need to have surgery to scrape those bumps off at some point."

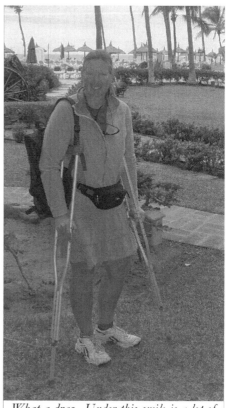

What a drag. Under this smile is a lot of frustration.

We hung out in Mazatlan an extra week, waiting... hoping... We had no idea what my knee would do. Would it heal to the point where I could ride? Would it continue to cause problems and we'd have to abort the trip? Should we abort now and not cause further damage? Day after day, our discussions centered around my knee as we tried to figure out what we should do. We were tired of hanging out and wanted to move on. And yet the consequences of a poor decision were severe.

In the end, we decided to move on. We waited until my knee was more or less stable and I could walk with a barely detectible limp. We vowed to ride very short distances the first week, at least, to see how my knee held up. The last thing we wanted to do was push it too soon and have it go out again.

Nearly three weeks after arriving in Mazatlan on the ferry from Baja, we were ready to attempt riding again. Our bodies had gotten soft from so long off the saddle, and we longed for the challenge of a good long ride. As much as we wanted to push on, we vowed to keep the mileage low, but we ended up even lower than expected.

Twenty miles out of Mazatlan we stopped for water in a tiny town called Quelite. As we hung around on the street corner filling our water bottles an old beat-up white pickup pulled up behind us and a voice boomed, "I heard you need help!"

We turned around to find an old American man with a red bandana around his neck and a backwards cap upon his head sitting in the driver's seat. "I was told an American family with two kids was down here and they need help. You need help? No? Okay. Well then, I think you should stay with me for the night." And thus was our introduction to Joseph.

The boys learned about mining gold from our new friend Joseph.

Once at the ranch Joseph jumped out of his pickup and unlocked the door to a house. "You can stay here tonight – it was being built for another American miner, but he died. The house isn't finished, but it'll be good for you."

And indeed it was. We wandered around exploring the six empty unfinished rooms. A thick layer of dust covered every surface. Water was from the hose outside, and there was a lone light bulb dangling from the ceiling of one room.

"Never mind those bugs up there," Joseph instructed as he pointed to a huge hive swarming with some type of small black bees directly above our heads. "They won't bother you if you don't bother them. If enough of them sting you though, they are poisonous and will kill you. During the night they are inactive, so don't worry about them tonight, just don't disturb them tomorrow."

We all looked at each other and made a pact not to disturb the hive.

"There are cots in this room," Joseph continued. "You need to use them – there are lots of scorpions and other bad insects around here. The state of Sinaloa has all kinds of nasties that you don't want to meet. If you sleep on the floor they'll crawl into your sleeping bags with you."

John and I began to have second thoughts about traveling through mainland Mexico. Should we really be dragging two little boys around an area with deadly bees and scorpions and whatnot? Maybe we should load the bikes on a bus and make a beeline for the USA, where everything was more familiar? But in the end, we didn't. If Mexican kids lived with those insects their whole lives, surely our boys would be fine for a few weeks.

We tried sleeping on the old dusty cots, but the burlap was so weathered and disintegrated, it ripped when we sat on them. Luckily we had our tent which we set up inside the old gold miner's house to protect us from the myriad of nighttime prowlers, and fell asleep wondering what our next day would be like.

Dear Grandma,

We finally left Mazatlan. Mommy says her knee is OK, so we are hoping we will be able to continue on. When we were riding an old gold miner named Joseph came and asked if we needed some help. He offered to let us stay in an abandoned house. In the abandoned house there were a lot of fold-out beds, a couch, and a lot of empty rooms. He showed us his gold-mining tools and machinery. He even showed us the mine! He grinds up the rock, then gets the gold out of it. The gold is found in some black sand that he gets out of the ore. It is neat. I can't wait until tomorrow.

Love, Davy

In my many years of traveling I've found adventure is, many times, only one step away from disaster. It springs from the unknown – from having no idea how we will meet our basic needs. It is stressful, but the kind of stress I can look back upon and say, "What an unexpected turn of events!" It's those days that make the most memorable experiences, and are, therefore, the most rewarding days of a journey. After it is all said and done, those are the days we look back upon and tell stories about – the days when we wonder where we will find food or water or a safe place to sleep. And Mexico provided quite a few of those days.

One day we had planned to make it to the next city and a hotel, but Mexico had this way of screwing up even our most well-laid plans. That particular day we had been plagued by flat tire after flat tire, and evening found us stranded on the side of the expressway with no place to sleep. Panic began to gnaw at our hearts. We were in the middle of nowhere, night was fast approaching, and we had been warned time and time again of the banditos who prowl the roads at night.

We could see, away on the other side of the corn fields, what appeared to be a small village. We had no choice but to head there and hope for the best. We hauled our bikes off the road and through the corn field to the group of houses. Our first stop was the store.

"We have a problem," I explained to the store keeper. "We had hoped to make it to Culiacan today, but we had a bunch of flat tires and now it's too late. The sun is setting quickly and it will be dark soon. We can't ride at night. Is it possible to set up our tent someplace around here?"

"The *jefe* (boss) will be here soon. You will need to talk with him," she replied. "He is inside."

We waited, knowing that each passing minute was one less minute we could be using to get to another village if need be. After waiting for what seemed like hours, the *jefe* appeared.

"Is it possible for us to stay here tonight?" I asked.

"You'll need to ask the social worker. She is inside," came the reply.

I was getting curious. *"Inside" what? What is this place?*

A few minutes later the social worker appeared and I repeated my question. By now we had a group of thirty or forty curious onlookers surrounding us while a small group discussed our predicament.

"They could put their tent in front of Miguel's house."

"How about a room? Could we give them a room?"

"The tent could go outside the fence."

Finally the social worker got out her cell phone and called the big boss to acquire permission for us to stay in the camp.

The four of us stood around, having no idea what was going on. They mentioned "the camp." What kind of camp was this? What was this place?

As soon as the social worked had permission for us to stay, she turned to the others and asked, "Which room should we give them?"

"They are so dirty. Which is the cleanest?" replied one woman.

Aurora invited us to stay in her humble abode in a migrant worker's camp. We were humbled by the kindness of people who had so little, yet welcomed us anyway.

"What about the office? Could we put them in the office?" suggested another.

Finally one of the women announced that, since she had two rooms, we could stay in one. The decision had been made. We wheeled our bikes into the *acampamento*, past dozens of wide-eyed curious kids, dirty run-down shacks, and people scurrying around doing endless chores. We followed Aurora to her rooms, which would be our home for the night.

The "camp" was for migrant workers from the south. They move north for several months to harvest peppers, tomatoes, eggplant, and corn, and return to their pueblos the remainder of the year. While working in the fields, they live in sheds made of corrugated tin. Doors are barely functional, light bulbs hang suspended from bare wires, and everything was filthy beyond description. Families of eight or nine crammed into one small room, and the shared bathroom facilities were barely tolerable.

Aurora invited us in and gave us a delicious dinner and a relatively clean place to stay. Davy and Daryl immediately hit the floor with Aurora's two children and the four of them stayed up half the night playing with a few broken toy trucks.

As I watched my sons roll around on the floor squealing in delight while they roughhoused with Aurora's kids, I couldn't help but think the world would be a better place if only everyone had this opportunity. For Davy and Daryl, it didn't matter that those kids didn't speak their language or that they lived in a dirt-floor hovel. What mattered was they were kids – and they could play together.

To isolate us from the heavily soiled mattress on the floor of our room, we spread our tarp over the mattress and used our sleeping bags rather than the blankets, but we weren't complaining. At least we were safe. After the lights were out and the camp was quiet, John and I lay in bed reminiscing about our previous adventures.

"This whole thing seems like a flashback," John told me. "Remember when we were in India? We would stop in a small village and were immediately surrounded by a sea of curious villagers? That's how I was feeling today – it was almost like I had returned to India."

"It reminded me of Ethiopia," I replied. "Remember when we were invited into *tukuls* of those people who were so poor? Even though they had no money at all, they gave us so much."

We continued talking well into the night about how it seemed like the poorest regions on earth was where generosity and the warmth of human spirit flowed most abundantly. We talked about cycling through the sprawling shantytowns of Calcutta where people lived in crowded, filthy aluminum boxes where running water was non-existent and there was hardly enough electricity to light a forty-watt bulb. We thought back to the refugee camps we had visited where the inhabitants struggled to maintain basic hygiene, or places where we cringed at the thought of eating in someone's home.

We couldn't help but feel overwhelmed by it all – by the kindness and goodness of these people who had so little, yet were willing to share what they had – and at our good fortune at being able to travel through it all.

Days later we were sitting by the side of the road minding our own business when an old, run-down pickup pulled up next to us with a full cab and a bunch of people in the bed. "You want tomatoes?" they asked. "*Por el viaje* (for the journey)."

"Sure!" I answered and began digging in my pannier for a plastic bag.

A man climbed out of the pickup, grabbed a huge gunny sack full of tomatoes, perched it atop my bike, and wedged himself back in to take off.

"Wait!" I called out. "We can't carry so much!"

The man climbed back out of the vehicle, grabbed fifteen or so tomatoes and put them in the plastic bag I had retrieved from the depths of my pannier, then threw the remainder of the bag in the bed of the pickup.

"*¡Que le vaya bien!*" they called as they drove away, smiles plastered on their faces.

Refreshments por el viaje - this family filled our panniers with oranges.

I stood there holding the bag of tomatoes and watched as the old pickup faded away into the distance. I couldn't help but marvel at the goodness of humankind; at how these people were happy to share whatever they had and asked nothing in return. I rearranged my panniers to make room for our unexpected treat and continued down the road.

A few hours later we were taking another break from pedaling, sitting next to a corn field. A pickup pulled up alongside us with a whole family sitting in the bed in lawn chairs.

"Want some oranges?" they asked. *"Por el viaje."* They started throwing oranges over the fence until the four of us stood with our arms full of oranges. *"¡Que le vaya bien!"* they called as they pulled away.

Dear Grandma,

We've had a lot of neat things happen lately. One night we stayed at a cheese farm. The people had a whole bunch of cows and we got to help milk them in the morning. The lady will take the milk and make cheese from it and sell it in the village. Some people offered to give us a whole gunny sack of tomatoes. We told him we couldn't carry it and got an amount we could carry. Later a truck stopped and offered to give us oranges. And boy did they give us oranges! We still have oranges. At least they didn't give us a gunny sack full of them.

At a toll booth there were some people selling sugar cane. Mommy bought a bag of it. Davy liked it, but I didn't. I did like watching them peel and chop it though. It was really cold this morning. Mommy wouldn't get out my long pants so I could be warm, so I had to be cold until the sun warmed me up.

Love, Daryl

We had heard so much about Copper Canyon and the Sierra Madre mountains that we couldn't pass by without seeing it. It was, however, way up in the mountains and quite inaccessible. There was no road from where we were so we toyed with the idea of putting the bikes on the train to reach the canyon. In the end, we decided to leave the bikes in the lowlands and go on a vacation from our bike trip.

Our next challenge was finding a place to leave our bikes. We headed to the train station to ask around

"Excuse me," I said to a worker at the train station. "We want to go to Copper Canyon, but need a place to store our bikes. Is there any place here at the station where we could leave them for a few days?"

He stopped to think for a minute. He walked outside to look at the bikes. "Talk to Jose – he's over there unloading those bags. He might be able to help you."

I headed over to the cargo area and explained our predicament to Jose.

"Yeah, you could leave them at my house," he told me. "That shouldn't be a problem."

We followed Jose across the street and down the road. We followed a narrow path through the rubble along a stream until we arrived at his house. John and I leaned our bikes against the side of his house while we went to see where we could leave them.

"You can put them right here," Jose said as we stood in his bedroom. "There is space right here along the wall."

We were stunned – this man was going to allow us to park our bikes right smack dab in the middle of his house for a few days. He calmly explained it would be absolutely no problem whatsoever and they would be perfectly safe – we could enjoy Copper Canyon without a single worry about our bikes.

You'd think that after all the bicycling we had done, and after taking the train up into the mountains without our bikes, we would have passed our time hiking or taking a bus tour. The last thing I thought we'd do was more bicycling. But we did. As soon as we got up in the mountains, we rented mountain bikes and took to the back roads of the Sierra Madres. The kids loved the freedom they never got on the triple – they could stop, start, turn and go as fast or as slow as they wanted to. For John and I, the best part was that all we needed to propel was the bike – not the hundreds of pounds of gear we hauled on our bikes.

It was spring in the Sierra Madres and the winter snow had nearly melted away leaving many muddy places in the dirt roads we were on all day. The roads led us through some spectacular wilderness as we passed through pine forests, numerous rivers formed by the melting snow, strange rock formations, and many hills and valleys.

We enjoyed cycling through the land of the Tarahumara Indians, indigenous people of Mexico who inhabited much of the land

The kids were thrilled with the independence provided by the single bikes we rented for them in Copper Canyon.

around Copper Canyon. One of the main attractions of the area (according to government tourist brochures) was these people. Since before the Spanish came they dwelled in the many caves formed in the unique area. The tradition of living in caves continues today, and we were fascinated with their dwellings. There were many caves scattered around, and all the rocks were totally covered with black soot from their fires.

A huge cave served as a several-family compound with side caves and crevasses made into individual rooms. The "courtyard," or central area, of the cave was where the women did most of their work and where social events took place. The Tarahumara women were very colorfully dressed, and we thoroughly enjoyed touring their neighborhood.

The kids were interested in the idea of people living in caves, but were infinitely more fascinated with the idea of their newfound freedom on single bikes. We took off for other adventures.

Dear Grandma,

We rented bikes today. It was fun. We went to Sebastian's Cave, where a bunch of people live in a cave. The road was a good dirt one, and I went flying. It felt good to be on a single again. When we got to the cave we went wild. We explored lots of caves and we found a patch of half snow, half ice. I was almost at the top of a rock hill when we had to leave. It was fun at that cave.

Then we went to Mushroom Valley. It wasn't actually a valley but it had big rocks in the shape of mushrooms. On our bikes we went up a rock that had a ramp on the side. Then we rode down. It was AWESOME!! I got on top of a mushroom-shaped rock with my bike.

After that we went to Valley of the Monks. We got some really fun pictures: one of me splashing through a stream, one of me going through a gully, and one of me holding a snow ball. It was very fun.

As we were leaving we found a baby lamb! Its mom wanted it back. Once the mom came walking toward us, but she got scared and headed back into the field.

On our way back to the hotel we went over some big hills! We would go up a steep climb and then drop down!!! It was awesome. It was undeniably, totally awesome.

We tried to rent a rowboat. We went over a rocky path to the lake only to find out they didn't have oarlocks. We were all very disappointed. Then we had to go back over the rocky path to get to the road. We were riding when we hit this kind of very squooshy mud.

When we got back on the road Dad said, "Let's fly like the wind!" So we did. And unfortunately some of the mud went flying right under my glasses and hit my eye. It hurt like heck. We made it back to town late in the afternoon. It was an incredibly fun day.

Love, Davy

As we sauntered along the rim of Copper Canyon the next day, it was almost as though I could hear a voice beckoning me from deep down in the canyon. Was it coming from the tiny villages dotting massive plateaus below us? Or maybe it was coming from the pueblos tucked in canyons, dwarfed by the towering cliffs on either side. It called me, urging me down to marvel at Indian villages isolated from modern civilization by seemingly impassable canyon walls – villages accessible only to the hardy souls willing to traverse precipitous trails leading to them.

Or possibly, the voice could have been emanating from the canyon bottom, lost and invisible somewhere below cliffs so high they seemed to reach to the heavens. It pleaded to me with a gentle, yet urgent, voice to go and discover its unseen mysteries.

I sat along the trail breathing in the rugged beauty of Copper Canyon and found it very difficult to resist the temptation to head off on a trail leading me down into the colorful wonderland. I knew, of course, there was no way I could heed the call. A couple of granola bars and a small bottle of water weren't exactly adequate provisions for the four of us to go exploring.

We contented ourselves with a walk along the rim past caves where several Tarahumara Indians, colorfully dressed in their traditional clothes, passed us on the trail as they went about their daily chores. We couldn't help but wonder about the civilization lost in the past – a culture nearly untainted by the modern world.

We reluctantly pulled ourselves away from the canyon and made our way to the train station to catch the train back to Los Mochis and our bikes.

Country Doctors

Finding a doctor in Mexico was always an adventure. It was one of those things that added a bit of the unknown to our lives. In the USA, finding a doctor was a fairly simple affair, and I'm sure finding a doctor in Mexico is simple too – for Mexicans. For an American with a sick kid, however, it was quite an event. In retrospect, it was quite amusing, but as I walked the streets of Los Mochis with Daryl whimpering in pain beside me, it wasn't much fun.

Daryl had been complaining of an ear ache on the train back to the coast, but he didn't appear too sick. The next day, as we hung around a motel readying our bikes for the onward journey, Daryl slept. When he awoke the following morning with both ears screaming in pain and with a high fever, I figured it was time to find the local doc.

With Daryl in tow, I asked a man outside our hotel where I could find a doctor.

"Just down the street there – across from the candy shop."

That sounded simple enough. Daryl and I set off to find the candy shop, but couldn't find anything remotely resembling anything like that. We found a video game shop, and an auto parts shop. We found a beauty parlor and a shoe shop. But no candy shop.

I stopped a woman walking along the road. "Excuse me, ma'am," I said. "Can you tell me where I can find a doctor?"

She looked at Daryl with tears streaming down his face. "Just go right around this corner and down a block. You'll find a clinic right there on the corner."

A few minutes later we walked into the clinic – into mayhem. In one corner a man gave a talk about dental hygiene to a group of *campesinos*, in another corner a group of clinic workers tried to figure out what to do with three huge sacks of potatoes. Scores of people milled around the waiting room, quietly talking.

I approached a person wearing a white uniform. "Can you tell me what I need to do here? My child needs to see a doctor." She looked at me with a puzzled look and directed us to sit down on the bench.

Somehow, we had managed to walk right into craziness – once again. This time we had managed to find a social services clinic, and no one had any idea what to do with us. The clinic was for poor people who needed the welfare of the state, not for American travelers. I could see them scurrying around, trying to figure out how to handle us, as Daryl lay with his head on my lap, moaning and groaning in pain.

After a few minutes a nurse came up and stuck a thermometer under Daryl's arm, then dragged him off to the scale. We eventually got in to see the doctor, and he prescribed some pain killers and antibiotics for Daryl's ear infection. They never did figure out how to deal with us on the paperwork side of things, and I suspect they simply didn't even record our visit, but Daryl was pretty happy about the medicine the doctor gave him.

We had entered Sonora, the wild west of Mexico. Towns and villages were few and far between, and mileage became crucial. We pedaled hard each day to make it to the next location with food and water. Day after day we pedaled hard, wearing ourselves down little by little. It happens so gradually, you don't even notice you're exhausted until one day – *blam* – you're hit in the face with weariness and exhaustion. It seems like those days come when you're least expecting it.

As we approached Guaymas, we had a choice – we could go into the city to stock up on food and water, or take the bypass around it. We were tired, and the thought of adding twenty miles to our day didn't appeal much. I stopped at a truck stop to make sure there were sufficient water and food stops along the road ahead, and the truckers all agreed there were plenty. Plenty for a trucker traveling at 50 miles per *hour* maybe. But certainly not for cyclists traveling at 50 miles per *day*.

So we rode hard, with little food and water. We did manage to find a tiny store at lunchtime where we bought tortillas and beans, and more tortillas and beans for dinner. As we were looking for a campsite, John got a flat tire, which translated to getting to a camp spot very late, eating dinner quickly, and collapsing in the tent.

The following morning we were totally wiped out. Too many days of hard riding, combined with not enough food and water, made us tired and grumpy. We only had thirty miles to Hermosillo, and we thought we could do that with our eyes shut. That was our first mistake.

For breakfast we each ate a tiny granola bar, drank most of our water, and headed out. A mile down the road my tire was flat. I unloaded all the crap from my bike and took the wheel off before remembering it had goop in it that should seal the puncture. I pumped it up, let it sit for a while to see if it would hold, then put it back on the bike. But with air in the tire it wouldn't go through the brake pads. We let the air out, put the wheel on the bike, and pumped it up again.

I rode about one hundred yards before it went flat again. Damn! I unloaded my bike for the second time, took the wheel off and took it apart. It was a gooey, slimey, icky, sticky, green mess! Goop was *everywhere*! Puddles of the green goo filled my tire. Using the very last of my toilet paper, we cleaned up the mess, hoped the tube would seal, and put it back together. I started pumping.

Now let me explain... Pumping tires up to eighty pounds of pressure with one of those little bitty pumps ain't no easy chore! So I got it up to about sixty pounds when I suddenly looked at John and shouted, "Fuck!" We had forgotten to put the wheel back on the bike before pumping. John let the air out so it would squeeze through my brake pads, we put it on the bike, and I started pumping again. For the fourth time.

By this point our tempers were short; about as short as they can get. We were exhausted, hungry, and thirstier than all get out. And that blasted tire wasn't helping matters. "You've got to hold the pump straight, Nancy," John exhorted. "Otherwise you'll break the valve."

"I'm doing the best I can," I retorted.

"That's not good enough. You'll break the valve." By that point John was nearly yelling.

"I said, I'm doing the best I can," I shouted back. "But of course, that isn't good enough for you! No! Couldn't be! Mr. Perfect himself!" I pumped with every ounce of strength left in my arm.

"Damn you!" John yelled as he grabbed the pump, still attached to the tire, and threw it to the side before storming away.

I looked at the tire and at the valve which was now hanging caddywhompus. "Now you've ruined it!" I shouted. "Thanks a bunch!" I yanked the wheel off the bike, grabbed my replacement tube and sat down to fix it.

John stormed over to me, grabbed the wheel out of my hands, and yelled, "Let me have it before you ruin it!"

Fine, I thought, *let him fix it.* I took out my book and sat down next to my bike to read. John set about the task of replacing my tube.

A few minutes later he was ready to put the wheel back on my bike but he wasn't willing to talk to me, and I certainly wasn't willing to offer my services to him. I sat on the ground while Daryl and Davy struggled to pick up my bike and hold it in place while John pumped up the tire. That was number five.

I meekly mumbled, "Thank you, dear," as I loaded all my junk on again. We had eaten the absolute last of our food, and drank every drop of water. We set our sights on Hermosillo.

Five kilometers down the road, my bike began to wobble. I looked down and saw... again. Same tire. This time a rock had worked its way through the tire and punctured my brand new tube. I unloaded my bike for the fourth time of the day, John took the tire apart, patched the hole, and I pumped it up for the sixth time. And then it hit – we had done it yet again.

We let out the air, put the wheel on the bike, and pumped it up one last time. I loaded the bike up for the last time, and set off for Hermosillo – tired, hungry, thirsty, and with my arm about ready to fall off.

Twenty-five miles later we pulled into the city and cycled to the very heart of it to find a hotel. I wearily went in to ask for a room while John and the boys waited outside. When I came out I found him deep in conversation with a woman while a man snapped photo after photo. We had apparently ridden right past the local newspaper and they chased us to the hotel. We were exhausted, filthy, hungry, thirsty, and wanting to collapse, but we stood around talking with the reporter while the photographer took a bunch of photos.

It was one of those days that I didn't want to remember. One of those days when I wished I could close my eyes, click my heels three times, and say, "There was no day like today... There was no day like today... There was no day like today..."

Dear Grandma,

When we were riding today Mom's tire went flat. Me and Daryl made up a game called box kicking. You get some boxes and try to hit the other person as much as possible. It's very fun. Then we switched to bottles. That made it more fun. Then we had to leave.

A while later the same tire went flat again so we stopped to fix it. We found more bottles on the ground and played again. This is how you play: You get some bottles and put them in a pile. Then you kick the pile to scatter them. You also have borders. If a bottle gets kicked out of the border you can go get it but you can't kick it at the other person, but the other person can fire at you. You can use your hands to block the attack.

OK, back to Mom's tire. Meanwhile, Mom and Dad were fixing the tire. They tried a lot of times to fix it. And after a long, long, long time, they finally got it fixed. That was a pain in the rear. Now the tire is holding good.

Love, Davy

The four of us pedaled northward into the Sonora River Valley toward the USA. As we drew nearer to our home country, excitement mounted. It wouldn't be long before we were back in our own country and we were all counting the days. As much as we loved Mexico, there was something about the US that was "home", even if we weren't at our house. The four of us agreed to pedal hard – we had four hundred miles to the border and we vowed to cross it in a week's time.

Mexico, however, had other plans. As we cycled into the Sonora River Valley, we were entranced time and time again by quaint, picturesque villages and old, historic churches in the area. We stopped to snap a few photos but pushed on, determined to make the mileage. Villages in the valley came every ten miles, each one more attractive than the one before.

Our third day in the valley, we pulled into Banamichi, intending to eat a quick lunch and continue on our way.

We made our way to the central plaza, leaned our bikes against a gazebo in the middle of the park, plopped ourselves onto a park bench, and began cramming sandwiches down our throats. Davy and Daryl, with their boundless energy, were soon up and running around with local kids while John and I took advantage of a few moments of peace and quiet.

A man approached and started telling us about the history of the region. Although interesting, what really got our attention was what he said next.

"Did you know there's a hot spring a few miles out of town?"

John and I looked at each other. A good long soak in a hot spring sounded pretty darn nice right about then!

"Another thing you might be interested in... There's a fiesta tonight over at the arena. They'll have a rodeo and music and *carne asada*. It should be pretty fun."

A soak in a hot spring sounded delightful. But a soak in a hot spring followed by a fiesta sounded absolutely heavenly. We decided to stay.

"We'll need a spot to pitch our tent. Know any place around here?" I asked him.

"Sure!" he responded. "I'll find a place. Let me get my car – you follow me."

We followed him down a hill and along a dirt road until he stopped at a ranch house.

"This'll be a good place for you," he pronounced as he climbed out of his car. "It has a canal so you can have some water."

He headed up to the house to ask permission for us. A woman and her mother-in-law came out, looking totally bewildered. I'm sure they had never had a bedraggled family on bicycles come ask to pitch a tent in their yard before, but they happily agreed to let us stay and we quickly set our tent up in their yard

We soon discovered the hot spring wasn't hot at all so we bagged that activity and headed directly to the fiesta. We could see the dust clouds hovering over the arena from a mile away, and could smell the *carne asada* a short while later. As we walked through the gates of the arena, smiling ranchers handed us bottles of Coke and Corona beer, along with plates of *carne asada* and beans. We drank. We ate. We talked with local ranchers. And all the while a joke of a rodeo went on.

John and I sat surrounded by drunk ranchers wondering if we had stumbled into a rodeo or a party. It mostly resembled a big party, but it also had all the elements of a rodeo: calf and horse roping, parading of horses, horse dancing and bronco busting. A ten-piece band played festive Mexican music while the crowd consumed ungodly amounts of Corona beer.

The four of us roared with laughter when it took a couple of cowboys a good twenty minutes to catch and rope a calf, and had tears streaming down our faces by the time one participant actually roped his partner rather than the horse he was attempting to lasso. The bronco busting was a complete bust when they put a cowboy atop a poor horse that wouldn't buck. We were in stitches.

Eventually the party broke up and we headed back to the garlic ranch where we had pitched our tent. Davy had been complaining about his hand since we left the plaza all those hours ago. Apparently he had slipped on an orange while playing with the local kids, and had watched the whole rodeo with an ice bag carefully balanced on his hand. As we were leaving the arena I suggested swapping out his mostly melted ice for fresh ice.

Within a minute, as I got a new ice pack ready, he started complaining. The new ice, since it wasn't melted, didn't surround his hand like the old ice water had and the numbness began to wear off. He started whimpering. Then he started crying. When he started begging me to cut off his hand I figured it was time to take him to a doctor, but it was late Sunday afternoon.

We arrived at the clinic to find it all locked up, but a knock at the door brought a doctor out.

"I think it's broken," the doctor told us, "But it needs an x-ray to be sure. Unfortunately, we don't have an x-ray machine here. You'll have to go to Ures to the hospital."

Davy looked up at me with panic in his tear-filled eyes. "Do we have to ride all the way back to Ures?"

"No sweetie," I replied. "Not on bikes. We'll take a bus or hitch a ride. I wouldn't make you ride seventy five miles with a hand like this."

Davy breathed a big sigh of relief, and the doctor started wrapping his arm in plaster. A few minutes later Davy left the clinic with an enormous splint extending from his armpit down to his fingertips.

"Remember – this is just to immobilize the arm until you can get to the hospital," warned the doctor. "It'll make it feel better, but you still need to get it checked out."

Somehow we needed to get to Ures. The doctor had said he would send an ambulance, but I figured that was a bit excessive. We headed out to the main road to hitch a ride. The first car we stopped just happened to be the rancher we were staying with.

"It's not even worth going now," he told me. "The hospital is basically empty on Sunday evening. All they will have you do is hang out and wait until tomorrow. Just go back home and we'll get you to the hospital tomorrow – we have to go there tomorrow anyway."

"You're going to the hospital tomorrow?" I asked. "Why?"

"My wife's father fell this morning and hurt his wrist too. We'll take him to Ures in the morning."

We turned around and headed back to our tent for the night. We had no idea what we would do with a kid in a cast, but we figured we would face that decision the next day.

The following morning, we got a totally unexpected reception at the hospital. Our photos had appeared in the paper a couple of times, and we were instantly recognized as local celebrities. Doctors and nurses scurried around trying to take care of us, and it wasn't long before we had the diagnosis – it wasn't broken, but very badly sprained. The doctor showed me the x-ray and I could very plainly see where the bone had bent, but not quite broken.

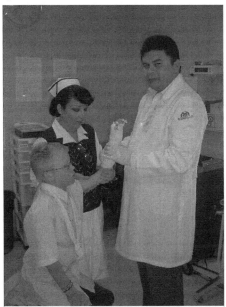

Davy severely sprained his wrist and wore the cast for two weeks. Fortunately he didn't have to steer the bike.

"I'll put a cast on it to make it more comfortable," the doctor told me. "It won't help it heal at all, but it'll at least make it so it doesn't hurt so much. And I'll try to cut it up above the knuckle so he can still ride his bike."

Davy and I had our doubts about riding with a cast, but we didn't have a whole lot of options at that moment. Davy held his arm up while the doctor began wrapping it with plaster.

"How should I record this?" a nurse asked. She was sitting at a rickety old desk in the corner of the room. "The referral came from the clinic in Banamichi, but he isn't *from* Banamichi."

Right about then the director of the hospital walked into the room to see us. "Don't bother with recording this one. Human rights – that's what we'll call it!" They didn't charge us a dime.

The following day was a challenge. The road passed through one of those sections where there wasn't a flat piece of road anywhere. We climbed. We descended. We climbed again. Steep climbs, followed by equally steep descents.

Before long, Davy started complaining of stomach cramps. He tried to help on the bike, but could only pull with one hand as the other lay protected in a sling. He kept doubling over in pain. John did his best to carry the two boys, but in the end, they ended up walking most of the climbs.

We made it thirty miles before deciding it was time to stop. By then it was after five, and we were pretty desperate for a place to put the tent. A major mountain pass was coming up and we figured it would be so steep we wouldn't find a place big and flat enough for the tent. We passed a dirt road, with a policeman right at the entrance. "Would it be possible," I asked, "for us to ride back that road a ways to find a place to set up our tent?"

"I have a little ranch right here," a grizzled old man who happened to be talking with the policeman said. "There is a nice flat spot in front of my *casita*. You can camp there."

We followed him up the hill and around the corner to his *casita*. And what a *casita* it was! At one point the three-sided structure had been built with mud bricks, but rain had washed them away until they were all heaped together in a jumbled up mess. The roof was patched together with all kinds of whatever he could find and held in place by old tires. Inside was barely space for a bed, with a few clothes hanging from the rafters above.

"I have a few cows," Ernesto told me as we sat around his tiny cookfire. He had built a wooden frame over the fire with a wire dangling down. He attached an old tin can filled with water from the river to the wire. Soon he would have hot coffee. "I sell them in town, but here in Arizpe they don't pay much. They only want the little ones for some reason, and the men from town take all the calves, put them in trailers, and haul them to the border. They get a lot of money for them there.

"I can't afford a trailer, so I have no choice but to sell them here in town. It would be nice if all of us small ranchers could get together and hire a trailer, but we can't all agree. We are stuck. We have no choice but to sell here."

"Do you have any kids?" I asked.

"No," Ernesto replied as he added another log to his fire. "I once met a woman that I really liked. She stayed with me for over five months, and I had hoped to marry her. She was three months pregnant with my child when her husband of thirteen years returned from the US and took her away. I didn't even know she was married. After that, I've stayed away from women."

We climbed into our tent and slept in comfort, while Ernesto fell asleep in his ramshackle hut.

Ernesto lived a simple life on his one-man ranch.

Yap! Yap! Yap! We were awakened the following morning by the barking of a multitude of dogs. I climbed out of the tent and saw Ernesto scurrying down to the river with a big pole. A few minutes later the dogs quieted down, and our host came walking up, proudly dangling a raccoon in front of him.

"Now what are you going to do with it?" I asked him.

"I'll cook it up – the dogs love eating raccoon," he replied.

"Will you eat it too?" I asked.

"Sure! Raccoon is very tasty with chile!"

Fortunately, we were gone by the time it was cooked.

Dear Mom,

Brutal. That's a good word to describe this wind. Last night we piled on every garment of clothing we could muster up from the depths of our panniers, mummified ourselves in our down cocoons, and spent the night listening to the tent rockin' and rollin' in the wind.

And yet, even being exhausted from fighting the wind, shaking from the cold, and uncomfortably crammed into my sleeping bag, there is no place I would rather be. Sure, I love those nice warm spring days with the wind at my back and easy terrain. But it is days like today that make me enjoy the nice ones so much.

Our journey is like a big pot of chicken soup – it just wouldn't be the same if you picked it all apart. Somehow each ingredient enhances the whole, making the whole pot a yummy concoction. That's how I feel about our journey – the good days and the bad days all meld together to make the whole. If I could somehow get rid of tough days, the journey just wouldn't be the same.

Love, Nancy

Unfortunately, it's impossible to capture headwinds in a photo. We were battling a howling gale right here!

I wrote that letter to my mom as I sat in our tent, wrapped up in my warm sleeping bag, refreshed from my night's sleep, and somewhat protected from the wind whipping around us. John and the kids were still sound asleep. I was dreading pedaling against the freezing cold howling gale all day.

Dear Grandma,

Jesus, Mary, and Joseph! It's cold! Yesterday we woke up with cold air outside our hotel room. We stayed there late because of the cold. At 11:00 we left. It was a miserable day.

We had a terrible day. We fought a very bad headwind. We made it to the intersection to Naco. There we found a part-worked-on house and we camped in it. It was a very, very cold night.

We only had one and a half tortillas filled with beans for dinner. The beans were cold because our stove wouldn't work in this cold wind. Then we climbed into the tent and me and Dad played Rummy before we went to sleep.

This morning I played two games of chess with Dad. One game we had a draw, the other game I won. We haven't gotten out of the tent yet, but I bet our water bottles are frozen again. I know I'm going to be tired tonight. We don't have any food except a few granola bars! We're going to be hungry till Agua Prieta.

Love, Davy

Battling an ice-cold headwind is a challenge. Notice Davy's face is wrapped in an Ace bandage.

The previous day we had fought a hellacious headwind all day, ended up out in the middle of nowhere with not much for dinner, and collapsed in the bitter cold for the night. And today didn't look any better. And yet, we were so close to the border we were determined. There was simply no way we were going to wait out the storm – come hell or high water, we would be in the USA that night.

If possible, the wind was even worse than it had been the day before. Daryl pulled his fleece neck gaiter up over his mouth and nose, we wrapped Davy's face with an Ace bandage and set out into the howling gale. Davy still had his cast on his arm (it would come off in a couple of days), so he couldn't pedal with full force. We fought for each and every meter we made.

It was a tough twenty four miles into Douglas, and then we had to turn back west ten miles to get to the college where a friend of a friend had invited us to stay.

But we made it back to the USA! We were "home" again.

SWAT Teams and the Unbeatable Foe

We expected the desert to come alive at night with animals, but in southern New Mexico it came alive in a different way. Nighttime was when hundreds of smugglers came out of the mountains separating the United States with Mexico.

We, of course, were clueless. We realized we were cycling right along the border, but didn't even think of smugglers coming across. All we noticed were the enormous numbers of border patrol vehicles. As evening approached, private vehicles diminished greatly and then vanished altogether while border patrol vehicles became more abundant. The road was deserted – no people, no houses, no trees, no nothing – except an ample amount of border patrol agents and a cycling family.

We pedaled along keeping our eyes peeled for a camp spot, but all we found was mile after mile of fence. Every once in a while we passed a gate, but they were all securely locked. Panic began to set in. We were cycling right along the border with

Mexico, the area teemed with border patrol agents, and we were desperate for a place to camp. It looked like we might be stuck for the first time since we left home.

We finally managed to find an unlocked gate on the south side of the road, hurriedly opened it, passed through, and headed back away from the road. We were half a mile off the road when a truck turned off the road and came toward us. We looked around to find a place to hide, but there was nothing. We stood still and waited for him to catch up to us.

"What are you folks doing?" asked the border guard as he rolled up beside us.

"We're biking through the area, and need a place to pitch our tent. We figured we would come back here. Is that okay?" I asked.

"You're doing *what*?" he blurted. "You're camping *here*? You can camp anywhere you want," he continued, "but this is a pretty scary area. There are lots of illegals coming through here. I don't want to say you can't camp here, but I sure wouldn't do it if it was me."

"Any suggestions?" I asked.

"I would think north of the highway would be a better bet."

"We wanted to go on the other side," I told him, "but it was all fenced in. We couldn't get back there."

"There's a road to the north less than a mile from here. No gate, no nothing. You could go there."

By that time the sun was down and we had precious few minutes of light left. We raced back along the dirt road, squeezed through the gate, and dashed along the highway. Just as we approached the dirt road heading north away from the border, a border patrol truck turned in. We followed them.

"Hi!" we greeted the agents in the semi-darkness. "We're biking through the area and need a place to set up our tent. Any suggestions?"

They looked at us like we were crazy. "Are you serious? You're biking *here*?"

After they recovered from the shock of seeing a family of four come out of the dusk on two bikes, they replied, "You'll be much safer camping right here next to the road rather than going back in. The drug traffickers don't hang around the roads because that's the most likely place for them to get caught. If they see you here by the road, they won't likely bother you. In fact, our truck will be right here – we're taking off shortly on the ATV's. If you camp next to our truck, the smugglers won't come anywhere near you."

We set about the task of setting up our tent a few feet from their truck, while chatting with the agents.

"You guys sure picked a winner of a night to come through this area," one of the guys told us. "There've been a lot of problems with drug smuggling lately, so we're on a major offensive right now." A helicopter zoomed past in the night. At least we assumed it was a helicopter – it was using night vision so all lights were off. "We've got hundreds of officers out here tonight – the regular border patrol, the Army National Guard, and we are from a Special Response Team out of El Paso. We're basically a SWAT team for border patrol issues. You're gonna have lots of activity all around you tonight – hope you can sleep through it!"

Davy and Daryl were fascinated with the idea of a SWAT team out there on the border. "What do you guys do?" Daryl asked.

"We save a lot of lives out here – that's mainly what we do. The US is putting more and more agents out here on the border and it's getting harder for the smugglers to get through, so they are leaving people behind. Basically, there are two kinds of smugglers: drug smugglers and people smugglers. The drug smugglers carry a backpack full of drugs and come across the border alone. We try to find them before they get to the road.

"The people smugglers risk a lot of people's lives. For each group of people wanting to come to the USA, there is one man – called a coyote – whose job it is to smuggle the group across the border. They start off in the evening on the other side of those mountains on the border – can you see them over there? Right on the other side of those mountains is Mexico. They set out in a group and cross those mountains. That's the easy part. Once they get on this side, they have to be very careful or they'll get caught. They pass through this valley and have to get all the way over to those mountains over there in the north – you can't see 'em in the dark, but they are about twenty miles away."

"Why do they have to get to those mountains?" Davy asked.

"They can't hide here in the valley – there's nothing to hide behind or under. If they tried hiding here, they would be caught and sent back to Mexico," the agent replied. "But the worst part is if someone can't keep up. The coyote won't tolerate anyone holding back the group, so they just leave the stragglers behind. Almost every night we find people out here wandering around. If we didn't find them, they would die. I rescued a mother with three kids once – the kids couldn't keep walking as fast as the others, so the coyote left the whole family behind and took off. The family was out here for two days before I happened to find them. Another time I found an old man who had fallen and sprained his ankle. They left him too. If the stragglers are lucky, the border patrol will find 'em, pick 'em up, feed 'em, and then send them back to Mexico. If they aren't lucky... well, at some point somebody will find a pile of bones in the mountains."

Davy and Daryl stood in awe of the whole situation.

"Want to check out our truck?" the agent asked. "We've got night vision on it which is pretty cool."

"Night vision?" the boys asked in unison.

"Here – look through my binoculars. You'll see what I mean." He handed Davy a small pair of binocs.

"Oohhhh!" Davy exclaimed.

"What?" Daryl asked. "What do you see? Let me look!"

The other agent took his binoculars off his belt and handed them to Daryl.

"Oh, cool!" Daryl shouted as he saw the green details of his surroundings through the binocs. "Look! Look, Davy! Look at the fence!"

The boys were in heaven looking through the binoculars at everything around them, while John and I set about getting the tent ready for the night.

Eventually, the agents had to get to work and we sat down to a dinner of MRE's (bagged meals designed for the military) graciously donated by our newfound friends, then crawled into our tent to settle down for the night.

A few minutes later the agents were back – with reinforcements. "Hey guys! Are you in there?"

John unzipped the tent and we headed out to see what was up. A group of five agents stood outside our tent.

"We've got something for you," one of them said. "We wish we had two, but none of us expected to find a couple of boys out here camping tonight. Anyway, we have this special collector coin that we want to give you boys. Each SWAT team has a special coin for their unit.

"When we get together with other units for training maneuvers we swap coins, and we try to collect as many as we can get. This is the coin from our unit." He handed Daryl the coin.

"Wow! Thanks!" Daryl exclaimed.

Davy was thrilled to receive a coin from the El Paso Special Response Team.

"Let me see! Let me see!" Davy insisted.

The agents smiled, waved goodbye and walked away into the darkness.

Dear Grandma,

We crossed the Continental Divide. It was very tiresome. It was an extremely long climb. We went up for about nine miles. It was a very gradual climb though.

Last night when we were desperately looking for a camping place, we found a road going south off the road. We went down it. A while later somebody told us that there was a very nice place to camp less than a mile up the road. We decided to try to make it there. And we did make it there, but we were surprised to see two border patrol men pull in. It appeared that they were patrolling the area.

They had lots of gear. They had four packs of bullets, a cool radio thing, a pistol, lights, and more! Their truck had four ATV's. They were prepared for anything. We chatted with them a while, then they gave us some MRE's for dinner. One MRE had a packet of Charms. The other one had a pack of Skittles.

Then they went for a ride on their ATV's. We had dinner after they left - it was good! Then a lot of border patrol men came and gave us one of their badges. It's cool. We got to look through infrared sensors. It was awesome! Then we went in the tent.

Love, Davy

By morning the agents were gone and we packed up and hit the road. It was a quiet day, the road was good, and we had a tail-wind. We flew along the deserted road in the middle of nowhere. Nobody... nothing... for miles and miles.

All of a sudden I saw a man walking along the side of the road. As we drew nearer, he started frantically waving his arms.

"¡Diez dias!" he shouted. "¡Diez dias!" He pointed to the mountains along the Mexican border. "¡Diez dias!"

"Wait a minute," I said in Spanish. "Slow down. Tell me what's going on."

"Ten days!" he repeated. "We got lost... my friend... still lost... maybe dead... ten days in the mountains... no food... no water... Ten days!"

I pulled a bag of bread and sandwiches out my pannier and handed it to him. He hungrily grabbed a sandwich and ate voraciously. John handed him a water bottle. He quickly downed the entire liter before returning to the bread.

"Thank you!" he said. "Thank you so much."

As near as I could figure it, he and his friend had set out ten days earlier from Agua Prieta, across the border from Douglas, Arizona forty miles away, ten days prior and promptly got lost in the mountains. They spent days wandering in the mountains, trying to get back to civilization. At some point, Jose's friend had gone down into a canyon to look for water, and never came back. Jose didn't know if his friend was alive or dead, but he continued on, desperately searching for some sign of humanity. He had managed to find the road just as we came by.

"Just stay on this road," I told him. "The border patrol will come by shortly – they've been passing every thirty minutes or so. They'll pick you up and take you to Douglas and help you get back home." I handed him a bit more water and a couple of granola bars for his journey.

I can't help but think he is one of the lucky ones.

It was cold and rainy. We were in western Texas where towns were pretty much nonexistent. The last thing we wanted to do was get wet and have absolutely no way to dry out. The little town of Cornudas would have to do.

I'm not convinced that "town" is the best word to describe Cornudas, but I'm not sure there is any other word. After all, it is a bona fide, certified town according to the books in Texas. But there ain't much there. Ain't much at all.

It was starting to drizzle when we arrived into Cornudas, and the skies showed no sign of clearing. We feared it would soon become a full-fledged rain and we were miles from a real town.

The great town of Cornudas consisted of a closed-down restaurant and a trailer for the groundskeeper. We parked our bikes under the overhang in front of the café and set about the task of waiting the storm out.

Waiting a storm out on a freezing cold patio was much easier said than done with two rambunctious boys. The boys had a grand total of ten feet across and maybe thirty feet long to run in and they quickly tired of the confinement. Within a few minutes of our arrival it was pouring rain, and there was nothing to do. It was too cold to sit still for long – our feet were numb within a few minutes if we left them on the concrete floor of the patio. We couldn't read for long – our hands froze in the frigid air. We huddled together on the benches, keeping our feet off the concrete in our attempts at keeping at least some semblance of warmth in our bodies.

"Hey look!" John shouted about three hours after we had arrived in our patio. "A truck!" Sure enough a truck went zooming past.

A short while later, he shouted, "A car! Look guys – a car!"

The boys became fascinated with the passing traffic. "A car!" Daryl called out.

"Here comes a truck!" Davy added a minute or two later.

"And look – another truck is coming!"

"I'll make you a bet," John challenged. "I'll bet more cars than trucks pass us."

"What'cha gonna bet?"

"I'll bet four cookies – two for each of you," he replied.

"You're on!" the boys cried. "There'll be more trucks – easy!"

All three of them ran to the edge of the patio and started waiting for vehicles. "A car!" John shouted. "That's one for me!"

"Yeah – but there's a truck!" Davy added. "One to one – a tie!"

"And another truck!" Daryl quipped a few minutes later. "How many need to pass before we win?"

"Whoever reaches ten first – cars or trucks," John explained.

"C'mon truck... C'mon truck," the boys chanted as they scanned the roadways. "C'mon truck!"

"Yay!" they shouted when a truck passed. "Ohhh," they moaned when a car came by.

"Three to one – my lead!"

"Three to three – we're tied!"

"Another car!"

"And a truck – woohoo!"

"Another truck!"

"Eight to eight," Daryl exclaimed. "C'mon truck! C'mon truck! We just need two more... C'mon truck!"

"Car! Car! Car!" chanted John.

"Truck! Truck! We want a truck!" the boys called. "Truck! Truck! We want a truck!"

All three of them hopped around at the edge of the patio, trying to keep warm as they kept their eyes peeled for traffic.

"A truck!" the boys shouted. "A truck! Nine to eight our lead. One more... One more... C'mon truck!"

"Something's coming! Something's coming!" Davy clapped his hands and hopped around in excitement. "C'mon truck!"

"It's a car... No, it's a truck... It's a.... Truck! Yay!" The boys ran around their small enclosure, jumping for joy.

You know you've sunk pretty low when the highlight of your day is counting the vehicles that pass. But in times like that... Well, it was preferable to sitting around getting even colder. The boys spent the afternoon counting cars.

By evening the four of us were wiped out. We huddled on the bench, shivering in the cold. We had pulled out our food and eaten a meager dinner. Setting up the tent on the concrete was unappealing, but outside on the grass was even less appealing – we really didn't want to get wet knowing we had a long way to go to the next town. John unrolled the tent and pitched it on the concrete floor of the patio under the overhang. Daryl crawled in and arranged the sleeping pads and bags. We tidied up the best we could and climbed in for the night.

"Hey guys! Are you there?"

I poked my head out of the tent to find the groundskeeper standing in front of us with a big tray of food. He had arrived back from town an hour before and had seen us hanging out.

"I figured you could use something hot," he said. "I brought you some soup."

"Soup?" piped Davy. "Hot soup?"

The four of us piled eagerly out of the tent and dug into the piping hot chicken noodle soup and hot chocolate.

"Wow! Thanks so much!" I said. "I can't tell you how nice this is. It's been a pretty miserable day hanging out here."

He smiled and walked back to his home, while we climbed into our tent with our bellies warmed and spirits lifted. Maybe it wasn't such a bad day after all.

Camping on the cold, hard floor under a restaurant awning was way better than being out in the rain.

"Where y'all goin' on them thangs?" a kid asked.

"Dallas," I replied.

"Y'all are goin' ta *Dallas*?" he asked in wide-eyed amazement. "On them ba-cycles? How long that'll take y'all?"

Upon our entry into town, we had picked up a group of kids who were fascinated by our bikes. They rode alongside us asking all kinds of questions.

"What do y'all do at night?"

"What about rain?"

"Do yer bikes get wet?"

We arrived at the grocery store in Lamesa and John and I left Davy and Daryl to deal with questions from the kid contingent while we went to buy our daily provisions.

"What about takin' a bath?" I heard as I walked away from the bikes.

Davy and Daryl did an admiral job answering the curious kids. By the time I emerged from the store a while later, Davy was off for a spin around the parking lot on a single bike he had managed to borrow for a few minutes. He came skidding up to us with a huge smile on his face.

"Do I have to go? This is fun! I wanna keep riding this bike!" He took off for another lap around the parking lot.

As we pulled out of town, the kids followed along, dropping out one by one, until we were down to only two escorts.

"How long y'all been ridin' those bikes?'

"How do y'all warsh yer clothes?"

Eventually, they decided they needed to turn around and go home. We continued on solo.

"I wish I could have my own bike," Davy grumbled. "That was fun back there!"

"Yeah – I'd like a single bike too," Daryl added.

Dear Grandma,

When we entered Lamesa we went to a grocery store like we usually do when we find a town. When Dad came out he brought a box of Zingers. We decided when we went fifty five miles we would stop and eat the Zingers. We had to pedal really hard because we were fighting the wind, but we made it. After fifty five miles we stopped to eat the Zingers. Dad told us the pack was $2.50 for twelve Zingers - that's a good deal! They were good! I like Zingers, but I prefer raspberry donuts. Those are better.

Love, Daryl

"But the real question is: Do you really want to ride a single fifty miles a day?" John questioned.

"I guess you're right. The triple's okay for that." Davy suddenly broke into a huge grin. "But can we get a single and tie it on top of the trailer?"

We woke up to very heavy fog. As we packed the fog thickened, and we stood around trying to figure out what to do. Even though there was a nice wide shoulder on the roadside, the dense fog led to very limited visibility and we didn't feel good about being on the road, but we also didn't want to hang out in our host's lawn for hours – he had been kind enough to allow us camp there the night before, but we certainly didn't want to impose any more than we already had. We headed to the local McDonald's to pass time until the fog cleared.

Our bikes were about as out of place in that small Texan town as a Martian spaceship would be on Pluto. As we walked into the restaurant with our shiny spandex shorts and cycling shoes, every head in the place turned to stare. Grizzled old men, their faces lined with wrinkles from the many hours they'd spent in the sun over the past several decades, stopped their conversation and sat holding their coffee, gawking at the spectacle that just traipsed in through the door.

"Where y'all comin' from?" inquired one of the men with a deep Texan drawl. He smiled at us with a big grin from under his wide-brimmed cowboy hat. He sat at a table with a group of men – must have been their Sunday meetin' day.

"Boise," John replied.

"Y'all come all the way from *Boise*? Did ya' hear that?" he turned to the other men at his table. "He said he come from Boise!"

The men shook their heads in wonder.

"Ya' come from Boise! Whar ya' headin'?"

"We're heading on over to Dallas," John continued.

"And then we'll keep heading east," I added.

"Y'all headin' to Louisiana? Whar to after that?" his friend asked.

"Manhattan," I answered.

"Manhattan!" he echoed in surprise. "How long ya figgerin' it'll take ta git thar?"

"How much halp are the kids?"
"Ain't that thang hard ta pedal up a hill?"
"How far do y'all go in a day?"
"What if you run into a ragin' thunderstorm?"
John and I answered questions until we saw the faintest flicker of sunlight flash through the window.

Cycling across Texas brought nothing but miles and miles of nothing but more miles of Texas.

We saddled up and headed into a strong crosswind. The only thing predictable about the winds in western Texas was that they blew all day long. We never knew which direction they would come from, but we knew they would be blowing.

"Just wait'll we get to Texas!" John had been telling us for months. "Once we reach Texas we'll be doing hundred-mile days *easy*! When I rode across Texas years ago I was doing a hundred twenty miles a day and not even pedaling. Just wait guys – you'll see! The wind'll be at our backs and we'll fly!"

We had been waiting for those easy, hundred-mile days for a long time, but hadn't seen them yet. All we had seen was wind. Lots of it. But it was never at our backs as John had promised. It came from the south and blew us over. Or it came from the north and blew us over the other way. Or it blew directly in our faces. But never, ever, did it come from behind.

Day after day we pedaled through the wide open spaces of Texas with nothing to stop the wind. No hills, no trees, no nothing for miles except miles and more miles of Texas. Thirty or forty mile per hour winds are enough to make cycling incredibly easy or phenomenally difficult, depending on their direction. Unfortunately, it seemed to always be in the "phenomenally difficult" camp.

The four of us hunkered down to fight the wind. Mile after painful mile we pedaled for all we were worth watching the mile signs slowly pass by. A few hours and not-so-many miles after we started out, I glanced over at the triple and my heart almost popped out of my chest. I looked at my boys, fighting the wind like the best of them, and my heart swelled with pride like never before.

In so many ways Davy and Daryl were typical nine-year-old boys. They sat on the bike licking their lollipops and telling toilet-humor jokes just like third graders everywhere. And yet in other ways they were extraordinary; so much more than other third graders. They had developed the strength and endurance to pedal hard for hours on end if needed, and the wisdom to know when it was. They had risen to the challenge of bicycling around North America. They never complained about cold or hunger or exhaustion, and they were a sheer joy to be around.

I realized that we had developed into a well-oiled machine; a team who knew and compensated for each other's weaknesses. We weren't parents and sons, adults and children, or teachers and students; we were all simply members of a team working together to fight the Texan winds.

We pulled into a rest area and John and I sat around complaining about the headwinds.

"I feel so cheated," John complained as he slumped into the bench. "We are *supposed* to have a tailwind in Texas. The wind *always* comes from the west around here. This just isn't fair. Every cyclist I've ever talked with talks about the incredible tailwinds they get in Texas. And yet here we are with these damn crosswinds all the time! It's just not fair."

Daryl came bounding up with a huge grin spread across his face. "You know, Daddy? The headwind is just part of the chicken soup!" He scampered away to play with his brother.

He was right. It was all part of the soup. Take it or leave it. Continue on or give up. There wasn't a gosh-darn thing we could change.

I had to dig deep – *real* deep. I burrowed down to the deepest depths of my soul to pull out every ounce of energy and every remnant of resolve I could find. Strong crosswinds, steep hills, and extreme exhaustion caused by far too many tough days in the saddle just about did me in.

We were racing a massive rain storm – and had been for the past three days.

"Y'all know thar's rain comin', don't 'cha?" the clerk in the convenience store asked.

We had heard it for days. Every time we stopped people kindly pointed out that rain was coming. Lots of rain. Three days of rain, in fact. The storm was behind us and closing in. We were determined to get to my high school friend's house south of Ft. Worth before it hit and were pushing mightily to make it.

Day after day we pushed on through the wind. There was no earthly way to consume enough calories to fuel our bodies for what we were demanding of them. We woke up early and stopped late in the afternoon.

As I cranked out mile after agonizing mile I chanted "Lillian.... Lillian... Lillian..." in the back of my mind. I couldn't wait to get to the small town of Lillian and my friend's house – even if I hadn't seen her for twenty-six years.

I had just about had it when we passed a sign informing us we still had twelve miles to Lillian. *Twelve* miles! Holy spotted bovine! Twelve more miles? I slumped over my handlebars.

John looked at me. "Do ya' see that sign, Nance?" He had a big smile on his face. "Only twelve more miles!"

I looked at him like he was nuts – like he had finally fallen off his rocker. He had finally plunged to the depths of idiocy. "*Only* twelve miles? Are you a stark raving lunatic? *Only* twelve miles? Twelve miles of these hills with this headwind is forever! Twelve miles of this is eternity! Twelve miles of these conditions is cruel and unusual punishment! Heck – twelve more miles of this is flat out torture! *Only* twelve more miles? Are you a masochist?" I fell off my bike and collapsed into the grass on the side of the road.

A few minutes later I somehow managed to drag myself out of the grass and onto my bike to propel myself those last twelve miles to Eileen's house.

We had done it. We had finished our mad dash to escape the rain. We had outrun the storm. At that point I couldn't have cared less when the heavens opened up. I didn't care if the cloudmen turned on their faucets and poured buckets and buckets of rain. I didn't care if it rained cats and dogs and horses and pigs. I was safely curled up in the cozy dry house of my high school buddy. Let it rain, let it rain, let it rain!

Dear Grandma,

We are at the house of Mommy's friend. We struggled a lot to get here, and when we got here we were exhausted. The family has three dogs, one four-year-old boy named Dyllan, and a whole lot more. Dyllan has lots of toys. He has a motorcycle game. He also has Thomas and Friends train set. He is a very big fan of Cars, the movie, and even has a Cars tent. We are having lots of fun here. We got to ride a go-cart. It was fun! But then it started to rain. It's been raining a lot. The entire yard is flooded because it rained so much. We are staying here longer than planned because of all the rain.

Love, Davy

Our week in Lillian had been wonderful, but it was time to move on. Days and days of pouring rain had flooded the region, but the roads were clear. The day started off great – cool temps, nice roads, and mile after mile of gorgeous bluebonnet fields. A tail-wind (blessed tailwind) pushed us along at a good clip, and the miles flew by.

By afternoon we started seeing flooded fields. Earlier in the day we had seen plenty of big puddles, but things had pretty much drained after the latest dowsing. By afternoon the situation changed. Huge fields were completely submerged and rivers and creeks were flowing furiously. It was actually quite beautiful with trees reflecting in the still water sitting atop flooded fields, but I felt badly for the many farmers who lost their crops.

"Mom!" Daryl called back to me as we pedaled along. "Did you see that?"

"Did I see what, honey?" I replied.

"The frog! The smashed frog in the road!" he called out.

We were accustomed to seeing dead animals on the road – cats, dogs, raccoons, skunks, coyotes, and armadillos. But that day the roadkill was of a different sort. The flooding had brought out frogs and turtles and snakes. The frogs were huge, and there were a couple of times when the front end of the frog had been obliterated, but the hind quarters were just fine. We could have picked them up and had fried frog legs for dinner if we had been the sort to enjoy that kind of thing.

By the time we needed a place to camp we were in the thick of the flooding. The road was raised, and therefore dry, but water extended as far as the eye could see on either side of the road. We pedaled eastward keeping our eyes out for a small patch of ground dry enough to set up the tent.

After what seemed like hours, we managed to find a field that was merely soaking wet – not submerged – and headed back to set up our tent in the muck.

Glooomp went my shoe as I pulled it out of a deep hole in the mud. *Gloock* went the other. As we walked around getting ready for the night, we left deep holes in the mud and ended up with soaking wet, muddy shoes. I pulled some crackers and cheese out of my panniers and balanced them on the rear rack of my bike while the four of us stood around eating dinner. Each time we moved, we heard the distinctive *glooomp* of the muck as we yanked our feet out of holes six inches deep.

Eventually we took off our shoes and dove into the tent, praying we wouldn't sink too deep in the night.

Very heavy rains had flooded eastern Texas. Fortunately, the road was raised, but camping in the muck was an interesting experience.

In the morning we packed up in the muck and yuck of the muddy field. The tent was drenched from heavy dew and everything that touched the ground immediately soaked up water. We couldn't wait to get out of Texas. We were tired of fighting the winds and tired of dealing with rain. We didn't hold out hope that Arkansas would be much better, but couldn't help but dream it would be.

We were exhausted. We still had many thousands of miles to go before we got back home to Boise via Connecticut, but not a lot of time. By our reckoning, we needed to pedal 1300 miles per month for the next four months in order to make it home before school started. Our average mileage so far in the trip was somewhere around eight hundred miles per month, but we vowed we would do it. The pressure was on, and it was taking its toll.

Mad Dash to Nowhere

We had crossed Texas. The route we had chosen had taken us directly across the longest part of the state. For nearly nine hundred miles we had fought the winds – mostly a crosswind coming from the south. Over and over we had questioned our decision.

Why don't we just turn north and take advantage of the wind? we thought.

But day after day we stuck to our plan and headed due east with the winds bowling us over.

So when someone suggested we turn north and head up to Missouri and the Katy Trail, the longest rails-trails in the nation, we jumped at it. After all, there really wasn't any reason we needed to stay south at that point. It was April and spring was upon us. We figured we would take advantage of the wind to blow us up to the Missouri River. After almost a thousand miles of fighting the Texan winds, we were finally going to get our just reward. We'd paid the piper and now was the time to cash in. We were heading north to let the winds push us for a while.

But the winds changed. We pedaled north against a headwind and I had to remind myself I was making chicken soup. But darn it! It was supposed to push us north! It just wasn't fair. The valley we were riding through was filled with the sweet smell of burning pine. It seemed like most houses in that rural part of Arkansas had a fire going, and for good reason. It was unseasonably cold and the strong wind created a brutal wind chill. The four of us bundled up with just about every scrap of clothing we owned and looked like the Michelin men riding down the highway. After a few days of balmy eighty-degree weather where we sweated all day, the cold was a bitter shock to our systems. Not only was it a shock to us, it was a shock to the people of Arkansas – it tied an all-time record set back in 1938 for being so cold. And we were headed north directly into frigid headwinds.

We were hunkered down, pedaling along the Arkansan highway when a car pulled up ahead of us and a woman jumped out. "I found you!" she exclaimed. "I came out looking for you guys – I'm so glad I found you."

She welcomed us to Arkadelphia, the "Peanut Brittle Capital of the World" and pulled out a bag of the sweet peanut-y concoction. "My cousin took your picture over in Texarkana yesterday and told me you might be coming my way. I thought I'd come out and see if I could help you in any way."

We were confused. "You came out looking for *us*," I asked, incredulous. "Huh?'

"Do you remember that man you met in Texarkana at the court house? He took your picture."

"Yeah, I vaguely remember him."

The courthouse in Texarkana is built on the state line. We stood with one foot in Texas and the other in Arkansas.

168

"He's my cousin," she told us. "He sent me your picture and said you might be coming my way – he really had no idea where you were headed. But he told me to go out and see if I could find you. It's going to freeze tonight, and he didn't want the kids out in the freezing cold. Would you come stay at my house tonight?"

Fifteen miles later we pulled up to Kathryn's house and peeled off our layers of clothes. She had a big pot of spaghetti and a smile as big as a freight train waiting for us, and we felt at home immediately.

After we had eaten enough to fill that freight train, the kids scurried off to watch TV while John and I sat around the table talking with Kathryn.

"So where are you headed from here?" she asked.

"We'll head north to Hot Springs tomorrow," John replied.

"Hot Springs? My daughter lives there!" Kathryn exclaimed. "I'll be heading up there tomorrow as well. My daughter and her husband are having a big Easter dinner – come join us!"

The following afternoon we arrived at Sonja's house in the early afternoon.

"Welcome! Mom said you would be coming. Come on in and eat – there's lots of food!"

The table was filled with ham and roast beef and sweet potatoes and hot fresh buns and more food than we had seen in ages. The four of us dove in and ate as though we hadn't eaten in days. Even though we had never met the people there, we couldn't help but feel we were home. Home on Easter – it was a good feeling, and one we wouldn't feel for a long time.

We had been fortunate for months – every time it rained we had managed to find shelter. Our lucky streak ended one night when we set up camp in a field and were awakened by the pitter-patter of raindrops on the tent. It rained on and off throughout the night, and we woke up to one of those dreary, gray days. We had no idea what it would do – it could clear up; it could start pouring

We sat in our tent debating what to do. Should we pack up and go, knowing we could very possibly get wet? Or should we hang tight, knowing that we had barely enough food and water to get us through that day, and certainly not enough to get us thirty miles into town the next day? John and I agonized over our decision. If we cycled, all four of us would need to pedal in shorts, keeping our one pair of long pants dry for when we stopped. But it was cold out – cold and wet. The kids would be miserable.

It was a crapshoot and there was no good answer. In the end, we decided we would be miserable no matter what we decided. We could hang out for the day, eating all our food and drinking all our water and be miserable the next day trying to get to town hungry and thirsty, or we could take off and ride in the rain and get wet and cold today. It didn't seem to matter which one we chose – either way was a bummer.

"Okay guys, here's the deal," John told the boys once we made our decision. "Tomorrow we'll be back to making chicken soup, but today it'll be poop soup. It'll be yucky and awful and miserable. But we're gonna do it. We're gonna take off and try to get to a motel. So, take off your long pants, put on your rain coats, and brace yourself for a terrible day."

The first five miles weren't too bad. No rain actually fell, but spray from the logging trucks was awful. We pulled into a little store and warmed up for a few minutes before setting out again.

A few miles later the skies opened up and freezing cold rain poured down. We made a mad dash for a carport of a nearby house. A woman came out and invited us in – she and two friends were having a quilting bee, so we hung out with them for an hour or so.

It was still drizzling when we set off, but we figured we needed to just go – it most likely wouldn't stop raining at all, and we hoped to make it to a motel. I felt like I was passing through an automatic carwash – rain from above, spray from my tires below, and spray from passing cars from the side. And it was cold – yucky cold. The kids were shaking and shivering, but never complaining. They knew that complaining would do absolutely no good whatsoever.

We arrived at a restaurant and pulled over. Four drowned rats piled in to eat. We ate, and then we sat. And sat. And sat, hoping the skies would clear. They didn't. With only a few miles left, we donned our raincoats once again and headed out into the pouring rain.

"Come in! Come in! Goodness – you must be half freezing to death!" The owner of a little hotel we had finally arrived at came out to shoo the kids in out of the rain and next to the fireplace. "You must be miserable."

The boys ran in happily, trailing a river of water behind them. It wasn't long before they were happily ensconced in overstuffed chairs before the fire with cups of hot chocolate in their hands.

John and I registered for a room, then headed over to turn the heat up to eighty degrees and run a tubful of hot water. We had camped out enough and were ready to pamper ourselves. I crawled into bed with a good book and John relaxed in the tub for hours while the kids watched TV. Outside the cold rain continued to fall. A hotel room never felt so good.

Dear Grandma,

Last night it rained. In the morning we couldn't decide whether to leave or stay, but finally we left. Once we started Daddy said he regretted that decision. I cried because it was so cold. Later it poured so we stopped at a lady's house. The rain was cold. The ladies were making a quilt. We stayed at their house for a long time. It was warm, but we couldn't stay there all night, so we had to go back out in the rain. When we finally got to the hotel the people gave us some hot chocolate to warm us up. I'm glad we came here even though it was miserable getting here.

Love, Daryl

John had become a slave driver. Every morning he dragged us all out of bed early, and cracked the whip all day. We were passing through the Ozarks, which are tough in the best of times. Long, steep uphill climbs followed by death-defying downhill plunges. Day after day we pushed on, wearing ourselves down. Each evening we dragged into a campsite, set up camp, forced down dinner and collapsed into bed. We no longer had the luxury of time to stop and smell the roses or play in the playground. We had to crank out the miles if we were to reach Boise before school started.

We were terribly behind schedule – we had hoped to be much closer to Connecticut by that point in time. Waiting out one storm after another had taken its toll, and fighting headwinds had slowed us down considerably. I began to realize I couldn't maintain that pace. I was exhausted. The boys were exhausted. John was exhausted – even though he wouldn't admit it.

"We need to go!" he urged. "We've got to make it 1300 miles each month! If we don't, there's no way we'll make it home on time."

I was quickly getting to the point where I didn't care. The joy had gone out of the trip and the magic was gone. We had reached the Katy Trail and I wanted so badly to enjoy it, but I wasn't enjoying it at all. We had arisen early and pushed all day. I could tell the Katy was a great ride – no cars, very gentle inclines, and nice scenery. The surface of crushed, hard-packed limestone was generally quite nice, but all the rain recently had softened it up a bit, making it quite sandy in a few spots. For the most part we were able to make decent time, but sometimes we went so slowly I felt like I could have crawled faster.

And then there were the flat tires. A few miles after starting in the morning, the trailer tire went flat. John took it off, repaired the tube, and put it back to together. A half mile later, his rear tire was hissing like a mad cat. A rock had worked its way through the tire, puncturing the tube. Changing the rear tire on the triple was a royal pain due to the drum brake, but we had no choice. We sat down in the middle of the trail and repaired it.

The flat tires and sandy surface had set us back, so we pushed hard to try to make it to where we had decided we would camp for the night. As the minutes ticked by and the sun made its way down, adrenaline kicked in and we screamed along the path at top speed, knowing the sun would bid us farewell all too soon. With nine miles to go, my rear tire went flat. I pumped it up and kept pedaling. I pumped it again at seven miles and at five miles.

In complete darkness we pulled into the city park in Pilot Grove to beg permission to set up our tent. Somehow, the gods were with us and we managed to find the right person – the man with the keys! He readily agreed to us camping there and even opened the bathroom for us.

We were exhausted. After pushing hard too many days, we knew something had to change. Davy didn't even make it to the tent before falling asleep.

We were all exhausted. For the first time ever the boys were too tired to play on the playground, and asked me *not* to read a bedtime story. Davy curled up and fell asleep on the park bench while John set up the tent. After carrying Davy to the tent and tucking him into his sleeping bag, I crawled into bed and let the tears flow. I was exhausted and knew I couldn't do it any more.

A New Beginning and an End

John and I both knew something had to change. We were too tired to continue. The joy was gone. The magic had disappeared.

The main reason for our trip in the first place was time. We were tired of the rat race of daily life at home and wanted time. Time to relax. Time with our boys. Time to smell the roses. And yet we had lost that. The daily rat race was back – different, but still there. We found ourselves pushing hard to make miles; to cover ground. We didn't have time to relax or enjoy our boys; we had to keep moving. We finally decided to escape from *that* rat race as well. We made the decision to slow down and enjoy the ride. We agreed to take time to play; time to learn; and time to smell the roses.

Our new plan called for an early end to the journey. Rather than the fourteen months we had originally budgeted, we would take only twelve. Rather than make a complete loop around the USA, we would stop in Connecticut at John's mom's house.

Our change of plans would give us time to enjoy our kids, but would also give us time with other important people in our lives. In our frantic mad dash to Boise, we had planned to spend a grand total of three or four days with John's mom in

Connecticut before heading out for the 2500-mile trek home. A change of plans would give us more time with her. And the news from Boise about my mom wasn't good. We decided to be back home in July to spend time with her before we started a new rat race of another school year.

In many ways our decision was tough – the death of a dream is never pleasant. But in many other ways it was a relief. In some ways it was not the death of a dream at all, but merely changing what was quickly becoming a nightmare back into a dream come true. We had come back to the beginning: spending time with our children exploring this grand country of ours – this place where we belong.

We changed our plans to give us more time to play - and play we did!

I felt like it was a new beginning. We stopped in Boonville for a couple of hours and didn't feel pressure to move on. We planned to stop early and camp in a conservation area, but somehow managed to miss it. In Rocheport we asked about it, found out we had passed it four miles ago, and actually pedaled *back*! We stopped hours before dark and enjoyed God's creation. We had made the right decision.

"Betcha can't catch that frog!" John challenged the boys. Davy dashed down to the banks of the mighty Missouri River... and returned a few minutes later covered with mud. Now, I'm not talking about that wimpy stuff we call mud in the west. This stuff was gloopy and gloppy, and thick as bread dough. This stuff wasn't just mud – it was plain ol' unadulterated Muck! Davy came up with Muck all over. The kid wasn't even a kid at that point – he was more of an ucky brown abominable snowman. John took one look at him and burst out laughing. "What 'cha gonna do now, Davy?"

Davy turned to me with pathetic, puppy-dog eyes and asked, "Mommy, will you help me?"

How could I refuse? How could I just leave the future of my genetic makeup standing there looking for all the world like a miniature Yeti. Bigfoot's child. I mean, one just doesn't *do* that to a child. You can't subject your offspring to the injustice of Muck, can you?

John's idea (which, in retrospect, was probably the better of the two) was to just let the muck dry and fall off in clumps. But I had other ideas – yessiree ma'am, I did! I would use the waters of the mighty Missouri herself to clean up that Muck. And my plan would have worked just peachy if my boys had had a lick of sense. But nine-year-old boys aren't exactly known for copious amounts of that commodity, and my boys were no exception.

I herded Davy down to the riverbank and Daryl, of course, followed. "I ain't gonna get in that river, Mom. No way!"

"You most certainly are, young man. Git yer clothes off and scurry your hiney into that water!" Davy stripped down and headed to the water – right back into the Muck.

Now Daryl thought that looked more fun than a barrel of monkeys, so he slipped off his shoes and ran to the river. "Don't get in the Muck with your clothes on!" I shouted a tad too late. Daryl sank to his knees.

I stood there on the banks of the mighty Missouri watching my two little boys slopping around, wallowing in the Muck. Those little guys were covered head to toe with ooey, gooey, mucky Muck - and loving every minute of it. "How on Earth," I wondered, "am I going to get these two out of here?"

One of my powers as SuperMom, I had discovered, was that of telepathic communication with my boys. Except that it didn't always connect the way it should. Maybe it was those nine-year-old brains that screwed it up... But somehow I managed to get them into the river to wash off and coached them on how to carefully exit the Muck on rocks, and we headed back to our bikes to continue on our way.

Cycling the Katy Trail was wonderful. No cars for over 200 miles!

I had forgotten how magic biking across America could be. In our haste – our mad dash – we had lost those moments; those moments of pure impulsiveness, of simple joys, of good times and laughter. But they came back once we made our decision. It truly was a new beginning.

Dear Grandma,

We finally had a fire this morning. We haven't had time for a fire for a long time! We made this thing we call "jets." It's when you get plastic on a stick and burn it. The plastic burns and drips down while burning and makes a really cool sound. Gallon jugs work the best. It was fun.

At lunchtime we climbed up a trail to the top of the bluff by the Katy Trail. I got a stick and crashed down bushes with it. When we got to the top Daddy tried to throw my stick down onto the trail we were riding on. It got caught in a tree.

When we were riding we rode over a snake. Daddy couldn't stop or we would've stopped on it and it would bite us. We couldn't turn or we might fall and it would bite us. So we rode over it. It was mad. When we looked back it was coiled up ready to attack. Then it slithered away.

Love, Daryl

We were pedaling along the highway a week or two later when I saw a sign: "Vincennes: 33 miles"

Hmmm... I thought to myself, *I thought Vincennes was in Indiana.*

We pulled out the map and sure enough – Vincennes *was* in Indiana. Which meant that we had nearly crossed Illinois. That's when the transformation happened. We were no longer just your normal, ordinary, run-of-the-mill bikers. Uh uh. No way. We were SUPERBIKERS! We were able to pedal as fast as the tail-wind pushed us; able to cross the state of Illinois in a mere three days. Yes, indeed, we were SUPERBIKERS! Okay, so I could have told myself that Illinois was an exceptionally narrow state, but I chose not to pop my own bubble. I chose to believe, for the moment anyway, that we had somehow taken on superhuman capabilities and could cross a whole state in less time than most people work in a week.

We had somehow made another seventy mile day. Although we had vowed to slow down and smell the roses, it was hard to ignore the tailwind. After so many days of fighting headwinds, we felt a *need* – an inner drive – to take advantage of every moment of a tailwind. So the wind was blowing, and we were pedaling – all day.

It felt great to have the luxury of making that choice. We had time if we wanted it. We could ride hard if we felt like it; we could stop when we chose to. It was a little slice of heaven and we reveled in the feeling of pedaling hard – knowing we didn't have to.

The following day dawned bright and clear. A tail wind pushed us along and we made good time. By noon, however, the sky lit up with the brilliant flash of lightning. I counted seven seconds before the ear-piercing crack of thunder exploded from above. It was only noon and it was dark and ominous. Another flash of lightning, but that time it couldn't have been more than four seconds before I could feel the thunder reverberate within the frame of my bicycle. We seemed to be heading directly into a violent storm and the blackened rain clouds above seemed continuously illuminated by flashes of lightning.

"Nancy!" John shouted to be heard over the din of the wind. "The storm is heading west. If we wait here I think we'll avoid the worst of it!"

BOOM! That time the lightning was right in front of us and flashed almost simultaneously with the roar of thunder. We stopped in the hope the storm would pass and we'd ride the last seven miles into town without getting drenched. After plastic bagging all our essentials the worst of the storm had passed and we continued on our way. Rivers of water

Preparing for a storm. Everything needed to be in plastic.

gushed down the sides of the road where just minutes before the storm had passed. We hoped we had managed to luck out again.

Unfortunately, with only three miles left it started pouring rain and, when we sloshed into town, we took shelter under the awning of a Dollar General store. The kids and I went inside to figure out where we might find a cheap motel, while John stayed out in the cold to watch the bikes.

A few minutes later John frantically beckoned us out. "Come here!" he called. "I've got a place to stay!"

A gray-haired woman with a gleam in her eyes and a smile on her face had driven up to John and asked, "Do you need a place to stay tonight? You're welcome to stay with us; we live right around the corner."

As the rain came ceaselessly down, we followed her home on our bikes. When we arrived, her husband was waiting on the porch to greet us, and he showed us to the basement where we would be warm and dry for the night. We couldn't have been more grateful.

The following morning we headed to the library to check email. Emails from my sister had become more and more frequent, with increasingly bad news about Mom. Cancer was ravaging her body and she was slowly, but steadily, getting weaker.

I clicked on the email from my sister and started reading. "I've been stoic for the past seven months, but now I need your sympathy. I am FRIED!"

As I continued reading, my heart fell. Mom wasn't doing well at all, and Glenda was at her wit's end. She was ready to crack under the stress. I needed to get home, and I knew I could no longer wait until July.

John and I discussed the situation and decided to abort our journey. We had known all along that day might come, and had agreed to head home if we were needed. Neither of us doubted we were needed now. Our journey was over. It had been a great ride, but now it was time to head home. We started figuring out the logistics.

We were in a tiny town in southern Ohio and there was not much there. There was no way we could have shipped the bikes home and it would have been a nightmare to try to find packing materials. We made the decision to ride to my other sister's house in Toledo two hundred fifty miles away. The way we figured it, we could get there in a week or less. It would take us a couple days to get the bikes packed and shipped. We would be home in Boise in ten days. The trip was over. We were going home.

Late in the evening, John left our hotel room to call Glenda on the pay phone. A while later he walked back into our room with a glum look on his face, and I knew the news wasn't good.

"Nancy," he said. "You need to go home – now."

"We are!" I proclaimed. "I'll be there in ten days!"

"No. I mean *now*. As in – you need to get home. You don't have ten days."

Mom had taken a turn for the worse. She had come home after a bunch of tests at the hospital the day before and had collapsed into bed. Glenda feared she would never leave her bed again. It was clear that Mom's time left on Earth could be measured in hours.

I felt so helpless. I wanted to *do* something. I wanted to rent a car and start driving. I wanted to get to the airport. I wanted to *move*, but I was stranded. There was no airport shuttle from the tiny town we were in. There was no bus. The rental car agencies were closed.

I wanted to make plane reservations, but I had no internet access. All I had was a cell phone with nobody to call. Nobody to call and make it all better.

So I sat. I sat on the porch of our hotel, passing the night... biding my time until morning when I could do something. I was utterly helpless and confused.

Morning came slowly, but once it arrived I burst into a flurry of action. I greeted the librarian as he opened the door and ran to the computers.

"Please help!" I posted on our online journal. "I need a place to stash my bike in Columbus while I fly to Boise! Please leave a message with my sister."

I called the airline and made reservations for later that day.

I reserved a rental car to get me to the airport.

While I was frantically making those preparations, John and the boys were at the hotel getting things ready for me. One bag to take with me to Boise; the rest of the stuff to leave somewhere in Columbus. Where I would leave it was anybody's guess, but we trusted that someone would come through.

A few hours later I was set – I had a rental car and a plane ticket. My bike was stowed in the trunk ready to be dropped off... where? I quickly called Glenda – she had been inundated with calls. In fact, one caller was on the other line at that moment. Yes, I could leave my bike in her garage. I got directions to her house and was off – off to see my mother one last time on planet earth.

We camped in every place imaginable - including a farmer's barn.

Dear Mom,

I look back through the years and think about all I've learned from you. You taught me to live, to experience and to grow. You taught me to love, to cherish and to treasure. And now you've taught me to die with grace, dignity and peace.

You taught me that I could follow my dreams – wherever they may lead – and you helped me understand the only limits I have are figments of my own imagination. I can reach for the moon – and if, for some reason, I fail to get there, I'll simply land among the stars. And for that I'll always thank you.

I've often stated you are the reason I could live the life I've lived. You are the one who gave me strength and encouragement to continue exploring our world. I know it wasn't always easy for you – when you thought I had been in that fatal plane accident in Guatemala, or feared we had been at the beach in Burma when the tsunami hit, I'm sure you fretted and stewed for days before learning I was safe. When I've taken off to the uttermost ends of the earth with little besides two wheels and a sleeping bag, I'm sure you worried with a smile on your face. I've said many times that you are to blame for my wanderlust – and I like to think you accepted that with pride.

Mom, you've been my strength – my backbone – for so many years. I can't imagine life without your quiet strength backing me up. And yet I realize the wheel must keep on turning. The circle of life must continue on, and some day my boys will be thinking about me – and I can only hope my legacy to them is as strong and wonderful as yours is to me.

I can picture you now, as you climb that final stairway to heaven. You pause halfway up and turn around to look back at me with a twinkle in your eye and your cane in your hand. You smile at me, nod your head, and say, "I'm fine" before turning to continue your journey. I hope that when my turn comes to pedal away into the great sunset in the sky my boys will say, just as I now say about you, "She's fine. Just fine."

I am honored that I have had the privilege of calling you Mom.

I love you, Nancy

The Fat Lady Sang

"Mom!" Davy cried excitedly when he saw me at the hotel in Columbus a couple weeks later. "You won't believe what we've done since you left! It's been a blast!"

"Yeah!" added Daryl. "We camped in an auction and Davy fell asleep at the Battle of the Bands and we rode dirt bikes and we went swimming and..."

"It was so much fun camping at the auction, Mom," Davy interjected. "There was tons of stuff all around and our tent was right in the middle of it! Daryl slept through a lot of the auction until Daddy had to wake him up to take the tent down."

"And last night we went to a Battle of the Bands – Daddy had to talk to the whole crowd! I got to watch him, but Davy fell asleep. I don't know how he could sleep with the music that loud – the whole room was shaking! I couldn't even go in that room 'cause it hurt my ears so bad."

"Today we rode up here with a whole bunch of people – Daddy said there were three thousand bicyclists! Can you imagine? Three thousand! We saw a quad bike! And they pulled a baby in a trailer behind them. We talked with them for a while. And there was so much food at the park! It was piled high – tons and tons of food!"

It was good to be back with my boys and good to be back to some sort of "normal." John and I had made the painful decision to carry on – there was no reason to abort the trip at that point. I had stayed home a couple days past the funeral to help sort things out, and then had flown east to rejoin my family.

John and the boys had arrived into Columbus about the same time I had so we met at a small hotel to get organized once again. I quickly reclaimed my bike from the wonderful people who had volunteered to store it for me, and we were together once again. My heart had a hole in it, but continuing on would help that heal.

It was already afternoon when we pedaled away the next day wondering what kind of adventures would come our way, and it didn't take long to find out.

"Hey! Come on over for some watermelon!" an old man called a couple hours later as we struggled up a hill in front of his house. "Take a break!"

We leaned our bikes against a tree and relaxed in his lawn chairs while enjoying watermelon, banana cream pie and ice cold water.

"Do you know anywhere around here where we can camp?" John asked Bob, our willing host. "It'll be dark in a couple hours and we need to start thinking about a place to pitch our tent."

"Yeah," Bob replied. "There's a campground six or seven miles up the road. Or, if you want, you're welcome to pitch your tent right here. I've got a big yard – it's not a problem at all if you want to stay here."

The four of us relaxed and enjoyed the idea that we didn't have to push on. We could ride ten-mile days and be just fine. We could afford the time to hang out if we felt like it and push on if we felt like it. What a luxury.

The following morning we set out to tackle the hills of eastern Ohio. We quickly discovered eastern hills are nothing like those in the west. In the west, where I'm from, we have mountains. In the east they have hills; I was used to climbing mountains. At home we always climbed up and up and up until we reached the summit. Sure, maybe there was a bit of up and down, but it seemed like we were generally headed in an upwardly direction – like we were making progress. We would crest a summit and descend – but not all the way – before beginning the climb to the next summit. We climbed a lot, descended a little, then climbed a lot again – with each pass getting progressively higher until we had crossed the mountain range.

In the east it was different. We climbed up and up and up, and then plunged back down to the same elevation we had started at. It was the Ozarks all over again, but this time we weren't racing against the clock. We settled into a rhythm and took our time.

By evening we were tuckered out and ready to camp. We pulled off the road and headed into a field.

I was awakened in the middle of the night by my husband. "It's raining, Nancy!" It was another one of *those* nights...

As John and I piled out of the tent into the blackness of the night, I vaguely remembered my thoughts as I trudged along the dirt road a few hours earlier. We had come upon massive mud puddles in the middle of the road as we headed back to set up camp. I had simply traipsed through the grass to avoid the mud, and thought, *I sure hope it doesn't rain tonight – this area will be one big swampy mess if it rains.* But John said he had heard the weatherman say it was supposed to rain tomorrow night, so I figured we'd be safe.

The weatherman was wrong.

We looked up at the nighttime sky through the few sprinkles of rain that were falling. It was illuminated by the near constant glow of lightning flashing off in the distance – so far away there was no accompanying roar of thunder.

"Whaddyathink?" John asked. "We could pack up right now and get to a motel before it really starts."

"Nah." I grumbled. "That's too much trouble. I just wanna go back to sleep. Let's just cover everything."

We put the fly on the tent and the tarp over the bikes and climbed back in. Fifteen minutes later the first gusts of wind passed through, followed shortly thereafter by the rain.

The kids slept peacefully, and I tried to sleep peacefully, but John kept waking me up.

"Are your corners dry, Nance?"

"Yeah."

"What time do you think we could check into a motel?"

"I dunno."

"Where'd you put the camera?"

"On my bike under the tarp."

"Are you trying to sleep?"

"I would be asleep if you would shut up..."

In the morning we awoke to pouring rain, knowing full well the field would soon be a swampy mess if the rain didn't let up. We sat in the tent contemplating an escape plan. The reality was there was no easy answer. It was muddy – dang muddy – all around. Any attempts at getting out of the field would result in a mess.

Heavy rains made for very muddy camping. It took us twenty minutes to clear the mud from our tires once we got on the road.

At one point the rain let up for a few minutes and we made our escape. We hurriedly stuffed the sleeping bags, packed the panniers, and strapped on the tent. It was only a hundred yard trek to the road, but everything was covered with gooey mud by the time we arrived at the pavement. Our tires were caked with layers so thick they couldn't even move.

John and I spent the next twenty minutes poking and prodding our tires with sticks to get rid of the worst of the mud while Davy and Daryl discovered polliwogs in the mud puddles. Then we continued on to town and checked into a motel. Sometimes a roof over your head is worth the price.

I remember reading stories about hobos when I was a kid. Hobos traveled around with their belongings wrapped in a bandana attached to the end of a stick which they flung over their shoulders. They were famous for hopping trains – waiting until the train slowly pulled out of the station before hopping aboard, then they'd hop off again as the train slowed to approach the next station.

John and Daryl spent our days traveling through the Appalachians perfecting the fine art of "triple hopping" – a strategy that helped tremendously with the hills. John couldn't carry both kids up the hills, so Daryl had to get off and walk. John wasted a lot of energy stopping halfway up the hill to let Daryl off. And then he had to stop again at the top so Daryl could climb back on.

Finally they came up with a plan – and perfected the fine art of "hopping." John figured out at precisely what point to give the signal to Daryl, and Daryl jumped off the moving bike to walk alongside. Then just as John was cresting the top, he gave Daryl another signal to jump back on. By the end of the day and after something like a trillion hills or so, Daryl could get off and on without John even feeling it. They had perfected their art.

That morning we had hit the road at 6:30 and after a tough thirteen hours of climbing hills, I was plumb tuckered out. We set off climbing yet another hill – and I just couldn't do it. We had hoped to make it another seven miles to a campground, but it didn't happen.

Halfway up a small hill, I stopped on the side of the road, panting, and collapsed over my handlebars. I was done.

I looked around to find a place to camp but we were right smack dab in the middle of a residential neighborhood. On one side of the road was a church, on the other a house with a man outside mowing his yard. A short ways down was a vacant field. The vacant field would have to do.

I approached the man on the mower. "Excuse me, sir!" I called. He came toward me and turned off the mower. "We're riding our bikes through these hills, and I'm exhausted. We had hoped to make it to the campground, but I just can't. Do you think anyone would mind if we pitched our tent in that field?"

"In that field? Over there?" He pointed to the vacant lot. "You don't want to sleep there – I'll tell you that for sure!"

My face fell. We would have to keep going. I had no idea how I'd do it.

"But you are welcome to pitch your tent in our yard here!"

John and I spent the evening chatting with Brian and Jackie, while the kids splashed in their pool with their daughter. It was the best end to a grueling day we could imagine.

All we hear about, it seems, are the bad people: drug dealers, suicide bombers, bank robbers, and murderers. By watching the nightly news or reading the morning paper, one would get the impression that our world is filled with bad people – people who would happily mug or rape or kill us. But our experiences showed us another side of our vast world – a kinder, gentler side where people were kind and generous and more than happy to give us a helping hand.

When we pedaled out of our driveway so many months before we knew we would find adventure. As we rode around our country we knew we would see a side of North America most people miss. And yet, all the random acts of kindness people offered astounded us. Each and every time someone reached out his hand and offered us help, we were humbled. It seemed like those experiences happened every single day.

The weatherman was not our friend again. He had called for a three-day rainstorm, starting that evening. John and I had come up with the brilliant idea of riding like mad to try to reach the ferry to Manhattan before the storm arrived. But, like most of our brilliant ideas, this one ended up being none-too-brilliant after all.

We pedaled away from some newfound friends' house bright and early, heading into New Jersey. We had 75 miles ahead of us to the ferry that would take us to Manhattan and some other friends' house. The hills weren't too bad and we pedaled like bikers possessed as we attempted to reach the ferry before getting wet yet again. We had made good time by early afternoon and stopped at a grocery store to buy sandwich stuff. When we walked out of the store a few minutes later the rain had started.

It was just a sprinkle at that point, so we bagged everything, put raincoats on the kids, and kept pedaling, determined to make the remaining forty miles to the dock. As the day progressed, it rained harder and harder until it was a pretty steady rain, and we were soaked through and through.

And then it happened – KABOOM! I wish I could tell you the boom was caused by something as trivial and inconsequential as lightning striking a nearby tree, but alas, such was not the case. My tire blew. *Boom!* Just like that. My tire was flopping in the wind.

We sat down in the puddles on the side of the road and attempted to fix it, but fixing it was easier said than done. The spare tube was way at the bottom of the trailer, and it was pouring rain. All of our essential gear – gear that absolutely could not get wet – was stored in there. Opening it up to get the tube would mean... well, it would mean wet sleeping bags and wet journals and wet other things that we would rather not face.

John attempted to patch the inch-long slit in the tube, pulled out our brand new tire that we had been carrying since Mexico, and put the whole thing back together.

I climbed on my bike and it wobbled like one of those Weebles things – you remember them? *Weebles wobble but they won't fall down.* But my bike certainly would have fallen if I got it over five miles per hour. It was pouring buckets, we were racing to catch a ferry, and my bike was threatening to go wildly out of control. I rode anyway – stopping every few minutes to pump up the tire that "more or less" held air.

A while later we pulled into the ferry parking lot only to discover that, on weekends, the ferry left from a different pier five miles away. And the last one of the day was leaving in thirty minutes. We took off like a herd of galloping turtles to see if we could make it. I pumped like a drowned mad woman on Mr. Weebles as I made a frantic dash to the ferry, with John and the boys trailing behind.

While stopped at a stop light, a black car pulled up alongside me, its window rolled down, and a face emerged. "Where are you headed?" the woman asked.

"We're trying to make the ferry! And it leaves in thirty minutes!" I replied as I took off through the red light.

Pedaling like mad through the torrential downpour, we crested the top of the second hill and readied myself for the final push to the ferry. The same black car pulled up beside me. "You aren't going to make it," she announced. "The ferry leaves in two minutes. There is no way."

My face fell and my shoulders sagged. I looked around at my dismal surroundings. Rain fell from the sky... puddles filled the road... we were soaked to the core, along with all our gear. This was about as bad as it gets. "Do you know where a hotel is?" I asked.

"The nearest hotel is about ten miles away. And it costs around $250 per night."

Life just doesn't get any lower than that. We were stuck in the pouring rain with our precious children in the middle of a massive urban sprawl. No place to pitch our tent... no hotels... nothing but rain and more rain. What kind of parent was I to subject my darling boys to conditions like this?

"Would you like to stay with us tonight?" she asked. "We live just a couple miles from here."

Once again, America's Road Angels had reached out and added magic to our journey.

On the ferry - it was pouring rain, but we were headed to Manhattan!

The following morning we loaded our bikes onto the ferry in the (still) pouring rain for the journey to Manhattan.

"Davy! Daryl!" John called out to the boys as they lay sprawled on the ferry floor. "Come here!"

The boys ran over to the window and the four of us stood enchanted – the Statue of Liberty was just barely visible through the rain. For centuries, Lady Liberty had signified a new life and a new beginning for immigrants as they arrived in the USA. For us, she also signified a new life – the end of our journey and beginning of a "new normal." Sure, we still had a hundred miles to pedal before reaching John's mom's house, but ever since we left Mazatlan, we had been telling people we were headed to Manhattan. And now, we were there. We had arrived.

I sat down in one of the seats to take a few minutes to contemplate it all. We weren't quite finished, but in my mind I was. New York City. Manhattan. We had arrived at long last.

"Did you hear the news?" the woman sitting next to me asked.

"The news?" I was startled out my reverie. "What news?"

"I was just listening to the news in the car before I got on the ferry. They said a massive downpour was supposed to hit Manhattan between nine and ten o'clock."

The ferry was scheduled to arrive at 8:50.

This time the weatherman was right. As we unloaded our rigs from the ferry, the onslaught hit. We toyed with the idea of hanging tight for an hour, but the call of our friends' house fifteen blocks away was simply too strong to resist. We headed out to fight morning rush hour in the torrential downpour with smiles on our faces.

After all we had experienced for the past year, the weatherman had nothing on us. A little rain – a lot of rain – never hurt anybody! And besides – we were here! We were in Manhattan! We laughed and joked as the rain came tumbling down and we pedaled through Times Square on our way to our friends' home. Life was grand. Just grand.

We were drenched by the time we arrived at our friends' house a mere fifteen blocks from the ferry dock in New York City.

We had hoped our last day on the road would be one of those glorious days when we sing with the sun, but instead it was pretty darn dreary. As we packed up one final time our song was accompanied by the pitter-patter of rain drops. By the time we took off, however, the rain had passed. We pedaled those last few miles on roads newly wet from the rain. Fortunately, the rain stayed just ahead of us for most of the day. About six miles from Grandma's house it began to drizzle. The four of us made a beeline to Grandma's, hoping to get there before the worst of the storm hit.

I never thought Union Station in New Haven, Connecticut was that big of deal – but somehow that first icon of "familiar territory" became a symbol for me. The trip was over. After a whole year of life in the unknown, I had entered into safe ground. I knew what to expect. I knew what was beyond the corner. And so it was all the way to Leetes Island. It was almost surreal – a feeling of being there, yet not quite comprehending that I was actually there.

When we took that final turn and started down into Leetes Island, I will admit to a bit of disappointment. I had somehow conjured up images of a red carpet laid out to welcome us home, a group of family and friends gathering together to celebrate with us. And there we were – in the pouring rain and no one was around. We stopped at the beach a few blocks from Grandma's house and I made John take the bike to the water for a "victory photo." It had to be the most pathetic victory photo ever. The kids were soaking wet and cold, and the absolute last thing they wanted to do was stand by the water for a photo; they wanted to get to Grandma's house and warmth.

But we made it, and Grandma welcomed us to her home. The kids were thrilled beyond belief. John and I weren't sure how we felt. It was done. The trip was finished. The fat lady sang and it was over.

Cold and wet, but we made it to Leetes Island! Grandma's house was just around the corner!

Changed Lives

In so many ways it seems like yesterday that we pulled out of our driveway so long ago with a whole year stretched before us like a vast prairie of time. Those 365 days lay ahead like an enormous red carpet welcoming us to new adventures. Eventually that prairie vanished day by day and the red carpet slowly rolled up to be stashed away.

Our year on the road continued to live in our hearts and minds and affected us in more ways than I could imagine. All four of us were indelibly changed by our adventure. We were touched by angels and beguiled by magicians' charms. We laughed and cried; we sweated and shivered. And we returned to Boise forever changed by our experiences.

As it happened, that year-long adventure was merely the springboard for yet another adventure on two wheels. We spent an intense year planning and preparing before taking off, in June 2008, to ride our bikes from Alaska to Argentina. It took us three years to complete that journey and the boys now hold the world record as the youngest people to cycle the length of the Americas.

Now that our wheels have stopped turning, we can look back upon our travels and see that they taught us more than we ever imagined. John and I knew our boys would learn a lot from traveling on bicycle – geography, history and science were built in to our lives, but their learning extended beyond the 3 R's of education. Sure their reading, writing, and 'rithmetic improved tremendously as their brains responded to the stimulation all around them. But the true legacy of our journeys is the "rest" of their learning.

One major thing Davy and Daryl learned is that complaining and moaning and crying don't help. If conditions are harsh, all you can do is keep your nose down and keep pedaling. Complaining won't change a gosh-darn thing. Davy and Daryl have learned to face adversity head-on and deal with it without complaining.

My boys also learned to think outside the box. I know no other children who've been so creative, so spontaneous, or so innovative about their playtime. Day after day, the boys climbed off their bikes in unique locations with unique situations.

Our family adventures forever changed all four of us. John and I were privileged with having the opportunity of being with our children 24/7 for a year – watching them grow and mature into responsible young men. Davy and Daryl have seen more of America than most Americans do in their lifetimes and have gotten to know people of all walks of life. There is no doubt in my mind that each of us is far richer for living this journey and that we've learned lessons we will help us on the rest of our journey through life on planet Earth.

Davy and Daryl learned that Earth holds no boundaries for them and they are free to wander wherever their imaginations take them. I hope they wander far.

It had been a remarkable year. We cycled 9300 miles through 19 US states and five Mexican states. More importantly, we had spent a magical year together as a family